THE SEVEN TOOLS

REDISCOVER YOUR CHURCH'S HIDDEN POTENTIAL FOR GROWTH AND VITALITY

DAVID ROSEBERRY

An RML Book (Read. Mark. Learn.)

An Imprint of LeaderWorks

ISBN: Paperback: 979-8-9863461-7-5

ISBN: Ebook: 979-8-9863461-8-2

+
RML BOOKS
LEADERWORKS
4545 CHARLEMAGNE DR., PLANO, TX 75024
PUBLISHED IN THE UNITED STATES OF AMERICA

❀ Created with Vellum

WHAT READERS ARE SAYING ABOUT "THE SEVEN TOOLS"

"The Seven Tools" by David Roseberry is a game-changer for ACNA churches. This concise guide offers practical strategies for growth using resources already available to every congregation. A must-read for rectors and vestries, it promises to reignite purpose and unlock potential across parishes. Roseberry's insights don't just promote church growth—they revitalize mission.

ARCHBISHOP STEVE WOOD, THE
ANGLICAN CHURCH IN NORTH AMERICA

With this most recent book, "The Seven Tools", Roseberry offers a masterful guide for church leaders seeking to cultivate vibrant, growing congregations. Well-grounded in Scripture yet responsive to our current cultural moment, this book provides a clear roadmap for fostering genuine community and cultivating a culture of discipleship.

DR. BRYAN C. HOLLON, DEAN/PRESIDENT
TRINITY ANGLICAN SEMINARY

"The Seven Tools" is a fabulous book. It is short, sweet, and to the point. I especially love that it is created as a guide for leaders and vestries to do deep and prayerful introspection to discover who God wants them to be rather than creating a punch list.

JOE PARK, PRESIDENT, HORIZONS
STEWARDSHIP

David is mature and wise, but he is also a whizkid when leading and growing a church. "The Seven Tools" is more than a to-do list or checklist. For instance, I don't think I have ever seen a church growth book that began with a chapter on compassion. The habits of leadership David commends are a living, breathing recipe for a healthy church that grows organically from its essential health. I commend "The Seven Tools" to every church leader, especially those unsure of what to do within a plateaued or declining church.

—BISHOP TODD HUNTER, BISHOP OF THE DIOCESE OF CHURCHES FOR THE SAKE OF OTHERS

This is vintage David Roseberry writing – clearly written, easy to understand, and difficult to put down until finished. Best of all, "The Seven Tools" offers encouraging advice and practical strategies for anyone seeking to reinvigorate their local church and turn it into a vibrant and growing congregation. Thank you for offering your readers another enjoyable and useful book.

MR. DAVID CHAPMAN, ST. JAMES, COSTA MESA, CALIFORNIA

Like a master carpenter training his apprentice, David Roseberry first identifies the tools that can build up a church and then shows from deep experience how to use them. My pastoral craft is improving under David's guidance; with this book, yours will, too!

THE REV. PETER JOHNSTON, RECTOR TRINITY CHURCH, LAFAYETTE, LA, EDITOR, THE ANGLICAN COMPASS

In a culture of church leadership that frequently emphasizes the newest, trendiest thing, Canon Roseberry has given us a reminder to keep the main thing the main thing and focus on the basics.

THE REV. CHRISTOPHER KLUKAS, ST. ANDREW'S ANGLICAN CHURCH, COLUMBUS, OHIO

In this excellent book, David Roseberry gives practical insights and tools that every Church can use to reach their community with the love of Jesus. I'm excited to have my team and key leaders read this with me.

THE REV. JOHN WALLACE, APOSTLE'S BY THE SEA, ROSEMARY BEACH, FLORIDA

David Roseberry has hit it out of the park again with his "The Seven Tools" book on nurturing a new or existing congregation into becoming the beacons of light each church is called to be in today's culture.

MS. SHARON FOX, AUTHOR, A PRECIOUS LIFE

I have read all of David Roseberry's books. "The Seven Tools" is the best and the most helpful of all. Most pastors never hear any of this in Seminary. As I read, I was only overcome with emotion twice. It's that insightful and personal. I'll be buying copies and using this book with my leadership.

THE REV. DALE CHRISMAN, RECTOR, TRINITY CHURCH, LAGO VISTA, TEXAS

David Roseberry's new book, "The Seven Tools", overflows with practical wisdom rooted in scripture and informed by three decades of church leadership experience. Roseberry calls us to look past the newest church-growth trends and reengage with what prepares a congregation to flourish in any generation.

THE REV. KURT HEIN, THE LIGHT OF
CHRIST, GEORGETOWN, TEXAS

Grab this book if you are a pastor, but don't read it alone. Read it with your staff team, leaders, and your board. This will give you a common starting point and prompt prayerful conversation to help you in your ministry context.

THE REV. DANIEL ADKINSON, RECTOR, ST.
THOMAS ANGLICAN CHURCH, ATHENS,
TEXAS

"The Seven Tools" is a treasure trove of wisdom gathered together over four decades of ministry that will be immensely useful to any pastor, regardless of their denomination. The good news of this book is that you already have all the tools you need to grow your church. Page after page, David invites you to pull those tools out of the drawer and use them to turn your church into a family heirloom that can be passed down from generation to generation.

THE REV. MICHAEL STRACHAN, RECTOR,
ST. DUNSTAN'S ANGLICAN CHURCH,
LARGO, FLORIDA

David rightly puts his finger on the idea that church growth, development, and renewal come not from the latest new idea but from using more effectively the time-tested tools every church already has. The tools in this book, well applied, will help the local church grow!

CANON MARK ELDREDGE, DIRECTOR OF
ANGLICAN REVITALIZATION MINISTRIES ,
AMERICAN ANGLICAN COUNCIL.

This easy-to-read, concise guide acts as a Swiss Army knife for building healthy, Gospel-centered congregations, providing essential tools for revitalizing ministry in today's challenging religious landscape.

THE REV. DR. JED ROSEBERRY, RECTOR,
RESTORATION ANGLICAN CHURCH,
RICHARDSON, TEXAS

FROM THE AUTHOR

As you might expect, I am humbled by the comments and encouragement from my ministry colleagues. I humbly ask my readers to read this book with an open heart and mind and then, if I may ask, leave an honest review on Amazon.

THE SEVEN TOOLS

CONTENTS

Let us consider how to stir up one another to love and good works, not neglecting to meet together, as is the habit of some, but encouraging one another, and all the more as you see the Day drawing near.

HEBREWS 10:24-25

THE ROADMAP TO REVIVAL

A PREFACE

Dear Reader,

I am truly excited for you to read this book. The seven tools I present in the following pages have the potential to empower you and your church to grow, increase, and thrive and to reach many others with the saving message of Jesus Christ. This book could be a roadmap to revival in your congregation.

If you are a pastor, church leader, or Christian layperson, you know the amazing power of the Gospel to change a human heart, heal a marriage, strengthen families, guide children and young people to adulthood, and provide fellowship, community, purpose, and meaning for all of life.

This is true for me, and it is true for you.

But there is a problem. Allow me to lay out the dilemma this book is addressing in three points:

1. You have experienced firsthand the Gospel's power to transform your life and to bring peace, purpose, and comfort

in times of confusion and hurt. You found the Lord—or he
found you!

2. There are many people around you who yearn for something
   that will bring healing, purpose, peace, and joy to their lives.
   They want what you have discovered. Though they may not
   know it, they, too, need to find the Lord—or be found by him.

3. And yet, strange as it may seem, many of our churches are
   shrinking, plateauing, aging out, and growing old and tired.
   People do not attend much. Visitors are few and far between.
   Membership is declining. Congregations are waning.

It is as Jesus said. The potential harvest is plentiful, but what is
harvested is not. Why is this?

*Our churches have members who love the Lord. These members know
people outside the church who are searching for purpose, belonging,
and assurance in their lives. With these ingredients for outreach and
growth seemingly in place, what's causing our congregations to
contract rather than expand?*

This is the question I seek to answer in this book.

WHERE THE ANSWER LIES

By God's grace and hidden in plain sight in your congregation are
seven powerful tools that can revitalize your church. These aren't revo-
lutionary techniques or complex strategies. Rather, they're timeless,
God-given principles that have built, sustained, and renewed congregations for generations.

This book is your guide to rediscovering and using these tools.

As you read, you'll likely recognize these concepts. They're rooted in
the natural hospitality and common sense that have been the hallmarks
of a healthy family and thriving congregations. This book's purpose is
to help you remember, sharpen, and intentionally use these tools in
your church context.

God willing, by the time you finish these pages, you'll have a clear roadmap for the revival of organic, numerical, and spiritual growth. You'll understand how to cultivate an atmosphere that not only proclaims the hope of the Gospel but embodies it in every aspect of church life.

THE SEED FOR THIS BOOK

But first, let me tell you where the idea for this book came from.

I was invited to conduct a retreat for the vestry or board of a church in a medium-sized city in the middle-south of the United States. The rector is a good friend and colleague who wanted to help his church develop a growing future.

Preparing for this retreat, I studied and made notes about what I wanted to say given the state of the broader church, our culture, and this moment. I considered the ministry and leadership experiences I enjoyed at Christ Church in Plano, Texas, where I served for over 30 years. I considered the wisdom I have gained from coaching a dozen pastors—they have taught me so much. During the Vestry Retreat, I took more notes as these faithful men and women reacted and responded to our discussion.

When we finished the day, I glanced over my notes and realized I had enough material to fill a book. And the strange thing is that we hadn't uncovered anything new.

We spoke about hospitality, friendship, volunteering, compassion for people, and the spiritual life of prayer. We also discussed preaching and music and how worship moves our hearts nearly every time we meet. We touched on deep friendships and small groups. And we admitted it was good to do what we were doing right then: retreating and planning.

I presented research about what people look for when they come to a new church. We discussed the time-honored practice of inviting friends, families, coworkers, and neighbors to Sunday worship. We also discussed the need for adult training and adult-oriented small groups.

Again, we didn't talk about anything new. In fact, we spoke about old things—things that have been a part of the life of churches over the centuries.

The rector dropped me off at my hotel early so I could rest. The following day, I was scheduled to preach. As I lay on the bed in my Hampton Inn room, reflecting on our productive day together, I couldn't help but think about notes I had presented and had taken, the pastors I've coached, and the countless churches I've consulted over my years as a rector and freelance church consultant.

I thought to myself: every church has everything they need to be every-thing God has called them to be. That thought is what led me to write this book.

In this book, I aim to remind myself, my colleagues, and church leaders that any congregation can become a growing church. I firmly believe that every church already possesses the necessary tools for growth, which is true of your church.

A BOOK FOR ANYONE

Any layperson, pastor, or church leader will benefit from this book. I am an Anglican pastor who, for 31, led a wonderful congregation in the North Dallas area; this book is not exclusively for Anglicans. I hope my colleagues will read this book, but it is not an Anglican book. Anyone can benefit from this book, the points I present, and the lessons learned from them.

This book, focusing on traditional church tools and practices, is for everyone: pastors, staff, lay leaders, seminarians, bishops, and adminis-trative leaders.

Whether you serve as a staff member, elected vestry leader, or on a governance board, the book can help reignite fundamental values that can revitalize your congregation.

THANKS BE TO THESE

The retreat prompted a series of blog articles on Anglican Compass, a popular Anglican website. Thank you, Peter Johnston and Jacob Davis, for whittling and carving the first drafts I submitted into manageable and readable blog posts.

Thanks to the thousands of readers who read them on the blog site. I was grateful to hear from more than a few of them.

When I saw responses to the blog posts, I imagined these posts could be reformed and rewritten to become the backbone of a more in-depth approach. They could be chapters in a book. These chapters are not blog posts with new tires. They have been reworked and expanded. I hope you feel they have been improved.

That was much harder than I thought. But I thank my wife Fran, daughter Taye, and my coach Victoria for cheering me on.

Finally, I sent this book to a group of rectors and leaders that I know and trust. That was the final litmus test. If they gave it a nod, it was good to go.

Their names are on the next page, and I am thankful to dedicate this book to them.

DEDICATION

For my colleagues, bishops, pastors, priests, laypeople, and fellow laborers for the cause of Christ.

Daniel Adkinson, Evan Baker, David Chapman, Dale Chrisman, Mark Eldredge, Sharon Fox, Bryan Hollon, Todd Hunter, Kurt Hein, Peter Johnston, Christopher Klukas, Joe Park, Jon Odom, Jed Roseberry, Michael Strachan, John Wallace, Steve Wood.

Feedback is the breakfast of champions.

THE ROCKING CHAIR, SEVEN TOOLS AND THE GOSPEL

MY ROCKING CHAIR

There's a rocking chair in my house with a unique origin. I built it with my own hands in a woodshop in Central Texas in 2008.

It's a piece of fine furniture featuring a modern, sleek design of hand-crafted cherry wood, created using traditional joinery and wood-working techniques. There are no nails and no metal screws. Instead, it has 45 mortise and tenon joints, each done by hand - my hand.

This project was a labor of love, taking over 100 hours—two full weeks of work. The woodshop where I built it adhered to a strict *"hand tools only"* policy. There were no power tools or computerized precision machines—just seven simple, rather old-fashioned hand tools: saws, planes, chisels, a mallet, drills, a square, and a workbench vise.

As I worked on my chair, I discovered the simplicity of this approach. There were no loud noises, whirring machines, or need for ear protection, goggles, or safety perimeters. All I heard every day was the sound of mallets pounding, chisels chiseling, and hand planes smoothing the surface of the wood. It was old-school craftsmanship at its finest. I'm proud of my work, and I think it might be passed from one generation to another after being called to my eternal home.

The craftsmen in the woodshop lived by a simple principle: *With just seven essential tools, a skilled woodworker can create virtually any piece of furniture.*

I learned that it was so.

Now, I want to transfer that idea, that 'vibe,' to the development and renewal of a congregation. That's what this book is about. It's about seven simple and effective tools every church has to build a renewing congregation that passes from one generation to another.

Just as I built that rocking chair with seven basic tools, I believe every church has at its disposal seven fundamental tools for growth, development, and renewal:

1. Compassion
2. Focus
3. Worship
4. Training
5. Small Groups
6. Community
7. Planning

These tools aren't complex or expensive; most are free. They're practices and efforts we use every day, anyway. The key is recognizing them, sharpening them, and putting them to practical use at a congregational level.

Your church has these tools already.

In the woodshop, we kept all our tools visible on our workbenches, not hidden away in drawers or cabinets. When I asked the master woodworker about this, he smiled and shared what sounded like an old proverb: *"Drawers and cabinets are where tools go to die."* I caught his point immediately - if you store something away, you forget you have it, and it dies a slow death of neglect.

The same principle applies to our churches. All the tools and abilities we have in our congregations are ours. They belong to us. They may have been hidden, ignored, deemed old, rusted, and discarded. In any case, many have been forgotten. But they are there. I promise this: you don't need anything to grow your church that you don't already have. That's because these tools are fundamental, intuitive, and deeply rooted in the mission of the church.

SEVEN TOOLS AND SEVEN PLANS

Transforming your church into a thriving, welcoming community doesn't happen overnight or by accident. It requires intentional effort, strategic planning, and a commitment to following the Holy Spirit's guidance.

So, at the end of each chapter, after focusing on one of the tools, you'll find a list of seven actionable ideas, suggestions, and considerations designed to help you implement the principles discussed.

This list of seven for each chapter is not meant to be exhaustive or even prescriptive. Instead, the ideas I present are starting points for your prayerful consideration and discussion. Not every suggestion will be appropriate for every church.

Please don't feel overwhelmed by the number of ideas! As a wise friend once told me in the early days of my ministry when I took on too much work, *"You can do anything you want, but you can't do everything you want."*

Let the lists inspire you to dream big, plan strategically, and act boldly.

VISITORS ARE VITAMINS

As you review these ideas, remember that new members and visitors are like vitamins to your church. They are an essential part of your congregation. They bring fresh energy and perspective, fortifying the body of Christ. This means your efforts to create a welcoming environment for new members and visitors will benefit every aspect of your congregation's life.

Change can be challenging, and it's important to remember that while everyone loves change, no one likes to *be* changed. The leader's role is to understand both the need for change and the appropriate pace of implementation.

Above all, keep your eyes fixed on Jesus, the author and perfecter of our faith. Trust in His guidance, rely on His strength, and believe in His promise to build His church. The times may be urgent, but our time is in the Lord's hands. Go confidently into the future as He directs and sends you.

LET'S REMEMBER THE GOSPEL

Before we discuss the tools for church ministry, we should remember the point of a church anyway. *What is the Gospel that makes it crucial for the church to proclaim it as Jesus's Great Commission?*

The term "Gospel" comes from the Old English "god-spell," which means *"good news"* or *"glad tidings."* It's a translation of the Greek word *"euangelion,"* which has the same meaning.

The Gospel is the climax of God's interactions with humanity and creation. The story begins with creation, where God creates a good world and places humans, made in His image, as stewards (Genesis 1-2). However, human rebellion (the Fall) disrupted this harmony, introducing sin and death into the world (Genesis 3).

The Old Testament unfolds as the story of God's efforts to restore this broken relationship, primarily through His covenant with Israel. The prophets speak of a coming Messiah who will establish God's kingdom and bring about ultimate restoration.

The New Testament presents Jesus Christ as the fulfillment of these prophecies. His life, death, and resurrection are the central events of the New Testament and the outline of the Gospel. As the Apostle Paul summarizes in 1 Corinthians 15:3-4, *"For what I received I passed on to you as of first importance: that Christ died for our sins according to the Scriptures, that he was buried, that he was raised on the third day according to the Scriptures."*

In other words, the Gospel is the good news that the God of love has acted decisively in Jesus Christ to rescue and renew all of creation. It addresses the fundamental human problems of sin, death, and alienation, offering forgiveness, eternal life, and reconciliation. It provides a new identity and purpose and calls all believers to participate in God's ongoing work of restoration.

If you are a Christian, this is the basic outline of your belief. Beliefs have implications and ramifications that impact every aspect of life, family, community, the nation, and the world.

This is the story of the Gospel, and it is the church's eternal mission to proclaim it, embody it, and call its members to live in light of it. Your church has this purpose. Through its ministry of Word and Sacraments, your congregation is an outpost for this work, and you are a citizen of the heavenly country we will all one day enter.

That's the plan, and that's our purpose. Now, let's examine the seven tools for getting the job done.

THE FIRST TOOL: COMPASSION

DEVELOP EMPATHY FOR OTHERS

Almighty and merciful God, whose Son, our Savior Jesus Christ, was moved with compassion for the crowds, seeing them as sheep without a shepherd: Grant that we, with hearts transformed by your grace, may share in Christ's deep love for the lost and the lonely. Inspire us to extend radical hospitality and share the hope of the Gospel with all who need a spiritual home. We ask this through Jesus Christ our Lord, who lives and reigns with you and the Holy Spirit, one God, now and forever. Amen.

As we explore the seven tools for church growth, we begin with perhaps the most crucial: compassion. But this isn't just about feeling for those in far-off places or abstract situations. True, Christ-like compassion starts right where we are—in our neighborhoods, across the street, and within our social circles.

I should say it unequivocally and simply: *if the people in your congre-*

gation do not have a compassionate and tender heart for those who do not have a church home, your church will not grow.

A church poised for growth is one where members understand that their compassion begins at home, or across the street. It recognizes that the people we interact with daily—our neighbors, colleagues, and friends—who aren't part of a church community need the Lord and the transformative impact of the church in their lives and families. This "nearby compassion" is the catalyst for authentic church growth.

THE LENGTHENED SHADOW OF A LEADER

While not a Christian, Ralph Waldo Emerson provided a striking metaphor for understanding the church. He wrote, "An institution is the lengthened shadow of one man." He meant that every institution comes to reflect its founder's heart, character, and nature.

In the case of the church, that man is Jesus Christ, and the founder's shadow is of deep compassion for the lost, the neglected, and the burdened. The institution that rose up around the teaching of the Lord, which would later be known as his bride, should, therefore, have this same compassion for the world—starting with those nearest to us.

In first-century Palestine, compassion existed but was often limited by societal structures. The Roman Empire primarily valued strength and conquest. Many Jewish religious leaders of the time viewed suffering as a potential sign of divine disfavor, sometimes attributing it to personal or hereditary sin.

Jesus introduced a radically expanded vision of compassion. He dramatically challenged the status quo. He reached out to the marginalized, the sick, and the outcast with a depth of genuine care that was uncommon and often shocking to his contemporaries.

A NEW ERA BEGINS

This wasn't just a new teaching but a seismic shift in how human worth was perceived. Jesus' compassion wasn't just countercultural—it was the dawn of a new era, where the last would be first, and the rejected would find acceptance.

As the lengthened shadow of Christ, the church is called to embody this kind of compassion. It's not enough to preach or talk about love; we must actively seek out those in society who do not know the Lord or who are not connected to a congregation in a meaningful way.

In a single chapter (Matthew 9), note the works of compassion:

- He heals a paralyzed man, moved by compassion rather than judgment.
- He calls Matthew, a despised tax collector, to be his disciple.
- He allows an unclean woman with a bleeding disorder to touch him.
- He brought a young girl back from the dead.
- He heals two blind men who beg for his touch.
- He frees a man from demonic possession.

And at the end of that incredible day, Jesus looked out on the crowds and saw even more work to do. He was indefatigably compassionate. He told his disciples the people were *"harassed and helpless, like sheep without a shepherd."* (Matthew 9:36). This moved the Lord's heart. This was the cause of his compassion.

In Jesus's view of the human condition, without God's intervention, people are beleaguered and burdened. Some versions translate it more dramatically: *"wearied and cast away"* or *"distressed and downcast."*

We know people like this. Many of us *were* people like this. But our faith changed us. Something happened in us. Or to us. We were different—maybe suddenly, maybe gradually. The Lord entered our hearts, and at the same time, we entered into his. We say, "We found the Lord!" but we also say, looking back on it, "The Lord found us!"

Which is it, we wonder? Who found whom? Does it matter? All we know is, as the Apostle Paul wrote, we took hold of that which took hold of us!*

WHAT DOES COMPASSION FEEL LIKE?

One of the first words most seminary students learn when studying Greek is the word for compassion. It is a difficult word to pronounce, and its spelling in Greek or English is nearly impossible. The transliteration is *"splangkhnizomai,"* which looks strange and forbidding. It is a guttural sound, onomatopoetic. It sounds like what it means: the turning and churning of the stomach or bowels. It is the opposite of what we might call 'butterflies'; it is a strong, deep, gut-level feeling of dread for someone.

Jesus felt this for these people. It wasn't a superficial emotion like pity or sorrow. It was gut-deep. That is why, after describing their condition, the Lord dispatched the apostles to do their work—or rather, to do the Lord's work through them.

COMPASSION FOR WHOM?

When I speak about compassion, I, of course, mean that sense of concern and empathy toward others we may not know or ever come in contact with. But I mean more than that, too. I mean to say that the compassion from your church members must be felt deeply for the people they DO know—the people in their social circles, friendship groups, dinner parties, working colleagues, gym co-members, and fellow parents at the neighborhood school.

A growing and thriving church is filled with people who care deeply

---

* This is the wording Paul uses in Philippians 3:12-14.

about the spiritual hunger in the depths of their neighbors—the people across the street. This nearby compassion is what drives church growth. It's about recognizing that the person you chat with at the coffee shop, your child's teacher, or the couple next door might be searching for the very community and connection your church provides.

At the core of any thriving church is a heart that shares Jesus' heart for others, a deep desire to see all people—near and far—connected to God. This same compassion should drive pastors and church leaders to prioritize reaching those who are disconnected from the life-giving community of their church.

In today's culture, which promotes isolation and individualism, people desperately seek a place where they belong, a community where they are known, loved, and supported through life's trials and triumphs.

Is your church that kind of place for you? If it is, you have what most people are looking for and what every person needs.

In other words, if your church is a community of people with whom you are friends—almost like family—and you feel safe and valued in your current church—*nearly everyone you know wants what you have.*

I can say it even bolder: The people you know in your social circles, work teams, work-out partners, friend groups, and the people you meet at an office, check-out lines, Uber rides, restaurant lobbies, or a coffee shop are all looking for what you have found in your church.

Why not show compassion for them and invite them to experience your church?

SURPRISED BY COMPASSION

Allow me to tell a story from the early days of our church plant when I first discovered that God uses tragedy and compassion to bring people to faith and community.

Like most homeowners in the mid-1980s, I made weekly pilgrimages to Home Depot on Saturday mornings. Once, as I walked toward the store, I saw a man walking out of a nearby McDonald's. I had nothing in my hands, and I saw he was carrying three or four large bags of food. They looked heavy, and the man looked distraught. I approached him and offered to help carry half the load. He agreed.

As we approached his car, I asked about the food. It was a lot of food. He said he had just bought three dozen Egg McMuffins. His eyes reddened when I commented that it was enough for an army. He explained that his teenage son was killed in an automobile accident the previous night. He was stocking up on food in case people came by. "I just can't bear the thought of needing to cook today."

I was heartsick and speechless. This man's pain seemed to invade me. I placed the bags of fast food in the back seat of his car, and before I closed the door, I reached out to shake his right hand. My eyes were red, too. I told him I was a priest starting a new church in town, and I offered to come by their home later. He accepted.

I met his wife and younger son when I stopped by the house that afternoon. Once inside their lovely, spacious, modern home, I spotted a stack of Egg Muffins piled high on a tray in their kitchen. They were untouched. Later, I learned the family was new in town They had just transferred because of his job. They moved into their new neighborhood a few weeks earlier. It was clear to me: they were alone in their grief.

I remember sitting in their kitchen, listening to the story about their son. They were eager to remember him to somebody. They shared a few photographs. They didn't try to hide their grief. They kept apologizing for crying in front of a stranger. They explained the tragic circumstances of the crash, the late-night visit from the police, the trip to the city morgue, the filling out of paperwork, and the long, silent, tearful ride in the early hours of the morning returning to their comfortable suburban home.

My heart broke for them. I was nearly speechless. Not knowing what to say, I asked if we could pray. (Thank the Lord for the several memorized prayers from The Book of Common Prayer.)

Before leaving, I asked for their contact information, and by day's end, I had mobilized other church members to provide support, meals, and pastoral care. Several members of our new church became their new friends that day and attended the funeral service later in the week.

That day a broken, grieving family found a compassionate church family and became members of a new community.

This experience sealed in my mind something that became a core principal for our new congregation. I wanted our church to be a place to preach the Gospel and worship our heavenly Father *and also* to be a compassionate community where a grieving family would never grieve alone.

YOUR CITY, YOUR COMMUNITY, AND YOUR NEIGHBORHOOD ARE FILLED with people with stories like this. They live near you, across the street. They work with you across the hallway. And you may even know them by sight or by name. If we are to stand in the lengthened shadow of our compassionate Lord and leader, then we must find every occasion to invite them into the fellowship of our community.

There comes a time in everyone's life when things happen, and people want what you have; they need what you have.

Remember, you are a Christian and you are a part of a community of people who know the love of God and who love one another and care about common hardships and joys. You have access to a community of compassion. Others deserve the same kind of compassionate community. And they are seeking it too.

When we truly embody Christ's compassion for our neighbors, colleagues, and friends, we become living invitations to the church community. This nearby compassion not only transforms individual lives but also fuels the growth and vitality of our churches, allowing us to stand firmly in the lengthened shadow of our compassionate Lord.

This leads to our second essential tool for church growth: focusing on our purpose to worship God and help others discover the Lord and his church. As we will see, growth is about increasing the number of people who find the Lord and find the goodness and compassion of his people.

COMPASSION—PARTICULARLY FOR THOSE IN OUR IMMEDIATE CIRCLES— is a powerful tool for church growth. These review points are intended to stimulate reflection and action, transforming your church into the lengthened shadow of our leader.

REVIEW POINTS FOR DISCUSSION

- Reflect on when your church provided crucial support during a difficult situation. How did this experience shape your understanding of the church's role in the community?
- Consider the level of enthusiasm among your church members. Do they believe in the church's mission enough to invite friends and neighbors to attend?
- As church leaders, how can we foster genuine compassion for the "harassed and helpless" in our community? What steps can we take to engage more effectively with our community's needs?
- What strategies can we implement to better equip our members to share their faith and invite others to join our church community?

SEVEN WAYS TO EMBODY COMPASSION AND FUEL CHURCH GROWTH

1. Create a dedicated group to identify and address immediate needs within the congregation and local community, serving as the church's first responders in times of crisis.
2. Initiate support groups for various life challenges such as grief, divorce, or addiction recovery, providing safe spaces for individuals to share their struggles and find support.
3. Create a sermon series and small group study centered on God's compassion, Jesus's ministry, and the Holy Spirit's transformative power in our lives and communities.
4. Provide regular times when church members can share their testimonies of redemption or restoration they experienced at your church.
5. Establish a team ready to assist families facing sudden crises, similar to the McDonald's story in this chapter.
6. Collaborate with local organizations to address systemic issues in your community, amplifying your church's impact through shared resources and expertise.
7. Create a program to support families moving into the area, helping them feel connected and supported during their transition.

Write your thoughts, ideas, comments here:

_____

_____

_____

_____

_____

_____

_____

_____

THE SECOND TOOL: FOCUS
ALIGN YOUR CHURCH WITH ITS MISSION

Almighty God, whose Son Jesus Christ looked upon the crowds with compassion: Kindle in our hearts a deep love for those who do not yet know you, and grant us the courage to invite them into the welcoming embrace of your Church. Help us to remember our own stories of faith and belonging, and inspire us to be contagious in sharing the life-giving message of the Gospel. May our churches be beacons of hope and belonging in a world that yearns for purpose and connection. We ask this through Jesus Christ our Lord, who lives and reigns with you and the Holy Spirit, one God, now and forever. Amen.

This book is predicated on the idea that every church has the tools to begin reaching new people immediately. The first tool is a heart of compassion—a deep desire that reflects the heart of our founder, Jesus Christ. Unless the people in a church see their unchurched friends and neighbors with compassion, the church will not grow. It can't. Ultimately, compassion is the source of all evangelism.

Compassion is the first tool, and it is paramount. And the second is like it: a church needs to remember who they are and why they started in the first place. It must remember its mission and purpose. This second tool is "Focus".

Focus, in the context of church growth, means maintaining a clear vision of a mission to reach and serve others, particularly those in the immediate community. It's about keeping eyes on the prize—the Great Commission—and not being distracted by internal concerns or complacency.

FIRST COMPASSION, THEN FOCUS

Compassion naturally leads to focus. When we truly have Christ's heart for the lost and hurting, we can't help but focus on reaching them. A compassionate church will instinctively direct its energy and resources toward fulfilling its mission of bringing people—far and near—to Christ and nurturing their faith in the local church.

As we saw in the last chapter, Jesus was moved with compassion when he saw the crowds, describing them as *"harassed and helpless, like sheep without a shepherd"* (Matthew 9:36). That compassion immediately led to focused action—he sent out his disciples to minister to the people. His focus was clear and unwavering.

Over time, it is surprisingly easy for churches to lose focus. As congregations grow and become more established, they can become inward-looking, forgetting their original purpose of reaching the people around them. This shift—or amnesia—can seriously impact church growth and vitality.

ST. JOHN'S CHURCH

Let me share a story that illustrates this point.

St. John's Church was once a vibrant congregation filled with the energy and passion of a new church. When they began in a storefront, the rector consistently contacted Sunday visitors, visiting them in their homes within the week. His dedication to building the congregation was intense. He canvassed neighborhoods, knocking on doors and sharing the news about the church and the Gospel story.

It was exciting!

I was later told about those early days of St. John's. Members recalled moving the "Greeting" part of the service to the end because it had become so lively and engaging; people couldn't stop greeting, hugging, and catching up with friends they hadn't seen in a week. Attendance and membership swelled, a testament to the strong sense of community and fellowship that had taken root.

But over time, growth slowed. Their upward attendance curve flattened, and the steady stream of visitors and newcomers dropped off. Their fellowship and sense of community remained as before, but something shifted. The church simmered down. After a season, attendance plateaued.

The rector contacted me, asking me to bring some perspective to the vestry to help the church get off its attendance plateau.

I arranged a time to visit St. John's, attending the Sunday service unannounced and without wearing my traditional Anglican clergy attire. I wanted to experience the church as a visitor and observe the warmth and hospitality I had heard so much about.

After the service, I stood near the coffee station, sipping the brew from a Styrofoam cup and observing the interactions around me. While I wasn't entirely ignored—a few people smiled at me—I was mostly left alone. The members seemed eager to catch up with their familiar friends but less inclined to reach out to a new face.

Later, I revealed myself.

They had set up a room with a few box lunches and enough members to create a loosely defined focus group. When I entered the room, I was greeted warmly by everyone. They now knew who I was.

We discussed the church's life, purpose, values, and short history. They were excited about their future. I didn't perceive any underlying conflict or hesitation to grow and welcome new people. I listened intently and took notes.

I had some things to ask them, but I couldn't overcome my experience of being overlooked or virtually ignored less than an hour earlier. I wasn't hurt, but I wondered what had become of their legendary friendliness.

I asked the group of them when they had last invited someone to the church. Could they give me the first name and the approximate date they had made their invitation? I was met with silence.

Not a single member had invited anyone in the last year! It was a sobering realization. I kept my comments about my incognito visit to a minimum, but their situation became clear.

I met with the Rector and Vestry the following weekend to share my first impressions and findings.

I put everything in writing, but this was the gist of my report:

- I told the vestry about my secret worshipper episode the week before. I told them how friendly the church members were— to one another. I shared that I had stood near the coffee station after the service and, while not ignored, I felt I was in the way of people wanting to greet the people they knew.
- I also reported asking the group when they last invited someone to the church. That was surprising. And telling.
- I also had to tell them more bad news: their church coffee was terrible. It tasted like, well, church coffee.

WHAT HAPPENED?

What happened to St. John's Church is a familiar story. After years of growth and accommodating new people, the members turned inward.

Inviting others and welcoming first-time guests had moved from being second nature to second place. It was a chore, a duty. The people loved their church and the people in it, but slowly, they shifted their attention away from the mission field.

And for good reason, too! At least in their minds. Over the years, most of their friends had become church members, and now the church members were most of their friends!

St. John's had been a church that existed to reach its neighborhoods, families, friends, coworkers, and members of the local community. It had succeeded for about ten years. But then it became a victim of its own success. People invited their friends, and their friends came and joined, and then they nearly ran out of non-churched friends!

The vestry and the rector faced a stagnant church that was aging out and failing to reach others. They had become an enclave of Christians who loved the Lord and loved each other, but they had forgotten their focus: others.

REGAINING FOCUS

After serious discussions and prayers with the vestry—we were on retreat—they committed to a plan, a course of action, to change the trajectory. The first thing they had to do was recover their purpose and focus.

Their pastor did the right thing. He provided the leadership with a place to talk, pray, and make decisions. He preached regularly about the community around the church, that they needed the Lord, and that only the Lord could answer the confusion and questions in our culture.

He also challenged his church to face mission-ward, trained his members to reach the people in their neighborhoods, and adjusted his calendar and time commitments to connect with visitors as he once did.

In other words, the pastor put the spotlight, focus, and energy on the people who were not members.

He later told me it wasn't hard work. Once people saw their friends, families, coworkers, neighbors, and the vendors and clerks they met day by day and remembered the compassion Jesus had for the crowds, they couldn't help but hopefully and confidently invite and welcome people into their church.

The rector told me of a compelling sermon illustration he used one Sunday. He announced that he had a long list of people in their community, and over half of them had no church to attend. Over half of the massive list of people, he said, would love St. John's if they were invited and attended. People were riveted. They wondered where their rector had found such a list.

Then, with a dramatic gesture, he charged his people to love their neighbors enough to invite them to enjoy the benefits of the Christian life at St. John's. And with that, he showed them the size of the list; he held a printed phone book in his hands. It made the point beautifully.

Within a year, the church recovered its focus and began to grow again. Recently, the pastor showed me a schematic design of a new worship facility they were planning to build.

What made the difference? The members realized that reaching out didn't mean venturing into unknown territory. They remembered their mission field included the people they already knew - their friends, coworkers, and neighbors.

The church continued its broader social outreach and ministry, but each member personally invited those in their social and friend circles. They recognized that loving others meant not just helping strangers they would never meet but also sharing the life-giving message with those they interacted with daily. This personal approach, rooted in existing relationships, proved powerful and effective.

THE ROLE OF LEADERSHIP IN MAINTAINING FOCUS

Church leadership is crucial in keeping the congregation focused on its mission. This involves consistent messaging, goal-setting, and strategic planning. Leaders must continually remind the congregation of their purpose and provide opportunities for members to engage in outreach and evangelism.

In the case of St. John's, the rector's leadership was instrumental in refocusing the church. He didn't just preach about outreach; he modeled it. He adjusted his own schedule to prioritize connecting with visitors, just as he had done in the early days of the church. This practical example inspired the congregation to follow suit.

OBSTACLES TO MAINTAINING FOCUS

Many distractions can cause a church to lose focus. Internal conflicts, financial pressures, or even success can shift a church's attention away from its primary mission. Leaders must be vigilant in identifying these obstacles and developing strategies to overcome them.

One common obstacle is the comfort of familiarity. As St. John's experienced, it's easy for members to become content with their existing church community and forget about those outside the church walls. Another obstacle can be fear—fear of rejection, fear of awkwardness, or fear of change. Overcoming these obstacles requires intentional effort and a renewed commitment to the church's mission.

FACING MODERN CHALLENGES

The turnaround story of this church might seem a little too storybook to be true. Some would say that the mission field has changed dramatically. We are not in Kansas anymore.

It is true. The church today finds itself in a vastly different societal and cultural landscape than it did just a few decades ago. The shift towards

a more secular environment has changed how people approach spiritu-
ality and church membership. The church doesn't have the cachet it
once did, and speaking to people about the Christian faith--much less
inviting them to church--could be dangerous!

That's all true. But despite these realities, the church's core mission
remains the same. And what is the heart-felt motivation for reaching
people? It is compassion, as we said earlier.

The fundamental human need for belonging, support, and community
persists. In an increasingly fragmented world, where many feel lost and
isolated, the church has a unique opportunity to offer a place of love,
acceptance, and family.

Do not doubt this. Ultimately, people need the Lord to sort out the
complexities of modern existence and find true belonging and
meaning.

People must learn to love others enough to invite and welcome them
into the church.

When a church's leadership is driven by a deep love for people and a
desire to see them experience the power of the Gospel, it creates a
ripple effect throughout the congregation. Members become inspired to
reach out to their neighbors, coworkers, and friends. They know that a
church family that shares their passion for seeing lives changed
supports them.

BEFORE MOVING TO THE THIRD ESSENTIAL TOOL, IT IS VITAL TO
understand the role of focus, vision, and mission in the life of your
church. Use these discussion points to review the chapter and reflect.

REVIEW POINTS FOR DISCUSSION

- How have you seen churches lose their outward focus over

time, and what specific steps can we take to maintain our passion for reaching others?

- Who first invited you to church, and how can you extend that same welcome to others in your social circles?
- Do you believe that being a member of your congregation would be a good thing for those who are looking for a church home or hope to find the fellowship and community you have discovered? Would it be a good thing for them? Then why not extend the invitation for them to come to your church?
- How does your church demonstrate love for those outside its walls, and what new initiatives can we implement to create a culture of welcome and belonging?

SEVEN WAYS TO REMEMBER AND MAINTAIN FOCUS

1. Conduct an annual Vision sermon series to reinforce the church's purpose. This series would help keep the church's mission at the forefront of members' minds and inspire continued commitment. Consider including testimonies from members who have successfully invited others to church.

2. Create a curriculum to help members discover their gifts and roles in the church's mission. This program would guide individuals in understanding how their unique talents contribute to the church's overall purpose. It should include practical exercises on how to share faith and invite others to church.

3. Implement quarterly check-ins with ministry leaders to ensure alignment with the church's vision. These regular meetings would help maintain focus and allow for timely adjustments in ministry strategies. Use these meetings to set and review outreach goals.

4. Develop a "New Member Orientation" that communicates the church's purpose and expectations. This orientation would help integrate new members into the church's mission from the start. Include a section on the importance of personal invitation and outreach.

5. Implement a vision budget process, aligning financial decisions with the church's core mission of reaching others. This approach ensures that resources are allocated in ways that best support the church's primary goals of outreach and evangelism.

6. Establish a "Vision Award" to recognize members who exemplify the church's mission in their daily lives, particularly in reaching out to others. This recognition would inspire others to live out the church's purpose in tangible ways.

7. Develop a "Mission Wall" to visually remind members of the church's journey and purpose. This display would help

connect current members with the church's legacy and ongoing mission. Include stories of how the church has impacted individual lives through outreach and invitation.

Write your thoughts, ideas, comments here:

_____
_____
_____
_____
_____
_____
_____
_____
_____
_____

THE THIRD TOOL - WORSHIP
CREATE SERVICES THAT INSPIRE AND EXALT

Almighty God, who has called us to worship you in spirit and truth: Grant that our churches may be places where all who seek you find engaging music, inspiring preaching, and authentic community. Give wisdom and courage to our leaders so they may be accessible and approachable, guiding us in the way of your truth. May all who preach your Word do so with conviction and clarity, leading the world to the transforming power of your love. We ask this through Jesus Christ our Lord, who lives and reigns with you and the Holy Spirit, one God, now and forever. Amen.

Attending your church is probably a habit. Sunday doesn't feel like Sunday unless you are up and headed to church for worship in the morning. If you have children in tow, you know that, though they might protest or resist, they will get with the program, get in the car, and sit with you in your familiar seat or pew.

But please consider what must go on in the heart and mind of a non-attender or a visitor to your church. What internal hesitations do they have to resolve to make a decision to join your church for a worship service? What preparations do they need to make the day before? What spousal objections or child reluctance do they need to overcome?

The dominant cultural expectation that everyone must attend a church has long since receded. It has become common for people to have no connection with a church or attend religious services. So, as we consider the third tool that every church has—Worship—please remember that if people come to your church to check it out, to explore, to visit, or because they have been invited, it means that there is something going on in their heart that is drawing them there. They could easily not go to your church, but if they are there, they are looking for something they think they might find.

WHAT PEOPLE HOPE TO FIND

A 2016 Pew Research Report gives us a snapshot of what people seek when they visit a new church.[*] Researchers asked a group of people who were not church members what they were looking for when planning to attend a congregation for the first time. Here is what the report tells us:

GOOD MUSIC AND PREACHING

The quality of music and preaching is one of the most crucial factors for new people. This is particularly important for liturgical traditions because so much of the service is the same week by week. However, these expectations are accurate across every denomination and size of church.

We should not be surprised that music and preaching should be at the

---

[*] https://www.pewresearch.org/religion/2016/08/23/choosing-a-new-church-or-house-of-worship/

top of a visitor's mind. Music is one of the most effective ways a church inspires and moves the human heart. And preaching the Word of God *should* be meaningful. (More about preaching later in the chapter.)

But we can draw this early conclusion: these two offerings—music and preaching—are twin engines for church growth, at least from a visitor's point of view. They are what visitors are looking for.

After over 30 years of leading services in a growing church, I've realized that for first-time visitors, music is more important than preaching. As a preacher, it's hard for me to accept this, but based on anecdotes, I believe it's true. Visitors have higher expectations for the music than they do for the preaching.

In a way, this makes sense. The visiting family might make allowances if a preacher has a bad day. They will imagine it was just an "off" day. (We've all had them!) But if the music is subpar—wrong notes, out of tune, slow, and dirge-like, it is hard to imagine they would want to return.

Why is this? Why do visitors react so strongly to sub-standard music? It is hard to say, but it's likely because most people are widely exposed to great music. Excellent music is everywhere. People hear outstanding recordings of their favorite music in their cars, workout routines, and home surround sound systems. High-quality music permeates our world so much that it is hard to tolerate anything else. Indeed, studies have shown that exposure to excellent music creates the desire for even *more* excellent music.[*] This makes sense.

In addition, music is repetitive. If the first verse is out of tune, people do not expect much from the second one. Music often occurs early in the church service—it is usually the first thing people hear—and sets the tone for the rest of the experience. People might think, *"Oh boy, if it's bad now...".*

---

* Peretz, I., Gaudreau, D., & Bonnel, A. M. (1998). Exposure effects on music preference and recognition. Memory & Cognition, 26(5), 884-902.

The quality of the sound, the clarity of the speaker, the reliability of the sound system, the effectiveness of the lighting, and the accuracy of the Scripture readings all contribute to the overall message conveyed to the attendees. In churches that use slides and overhead projection, missteps such as out-of-sync slides or incorrect slides are distracting; they detract from the worship experience. These issues cause frustration for the congregation and lead to missed opportunities for meaningful worship.

Technical aspects, while seemingly minor, can significantly impact a visitor's experience. While people love their church, mediocrity is sure to impact their willingness to invite a friend. A church serious about growth *must* pay attention to these details, ensuring that these issues support, rather than hinder, the worship experience.

Put plainly, a worship service that is unrehearsed, led by people who are unprepared, and using technology that is unreliable, will leave visitors underwhelmed and members understandably hesitant to invite others.

A PLACE TO MEET NEW FRIENDS

According to the research survey, visitors also expect a church to be a place to meet new friends. The best metaphor for most congregations is a community or a family, and people want to be a part of one. People want good friends, and a church should be the place to find them.

This was the culture of the earliest Christians. They were closely connected friends.

For example, one of the least known aspects of the Apostle Paul's nature is hiding in plain sight in the New Testament. From the first day of his conversion, when he was escorted into the city of Damascus and cared for in a private residence, to the last days of his life in a prison cell in Rome, the unobserved fact about Paul's life is his vast number of friends. Some 70-plus different names are mentioned in his letters, making Paul the friendliest man in the Bible.

Paul knew these people. He loved them. In most letters, he sends his greetings, well-wishes, and personal updates throughout the church. Upon his conversion, Paul discovered that one of the main features of being a Christian was that, along with the friendship and love of the Living Lord Jesus and the assurance of eternal life, you had a widespread, welcoming community where people knew your name and provided the things in life that make it worth living: tenderness, prayer, caring, warmth, support, food, encouragement, and love.

Sadly, our churches often do not see themselves as friendship factories, but they could be. People are looking for good friends with whom they can share their lives, the challenges, and the transitions, joys, and sorrows of modern life.

A church should do everything possible to facilitate friendships where people are known by their names. We will discuss this later in the book.

HOLY COMMUNION

The Eucharist, when offered with sincerity and conviction, has the power to transcend mere ritual and touch hearts in ways that music and preaching alone cannot. It provides a tangible connection to the divine and a sense of community that many seekers crave.

However, like other aspects of the service, the administration of Communion must be handled with care and reverence. A rushed or perfunctory Eucharist can feel hollow and meaningless to both visitors and regular attendees. On the other hand, when presented with dignity and explained thoughtfully, it can become a transformative moment that draws visitors deeper into the church's life.

Leaders should communicate the importance of this sacramental experience clearly, inviting baptized people to participate while respecting that some may not want to because they are not Christians. But even if people do not fully participate in the Communion service, we want them to sense its importance and sacredness; we want them to drive home knowing that they have been to something sacred.

SPEAKING OF PREACHING

Studies indicate that the quality of preaching is the primary factor people consider when selecting a new church. This aligns with my deeply held belief: *There is no greater gift we can offer to Sunday morning visitors than a sermon rooted in the Word of God.*

Of course, it is not a time for a spotlight to shine on the preacher. That's not what makes preaching important. It is not about being folksy, relatable, humorous, or a good storyteller. Those skills and preaching styles are important and can be developed over time. The sermon—that 20-30 minute period when the preacher expounds the Word of God—is when the preacher does something for the visitors and attendees that no one else will ever do: *tell them the truth about God's Word.*

Consider the act of preaching from a visitor's point of view.

The newcomer walks into the congregation and sees many things happening around them. They hear music, sing songs, listen to a reading, and read a Psalm. They stand. They sit. They kneel. They greet one another.

But then, for an all-too-short period of time, they listen to an expert in the knowledge of God speak to them about what the Bible has to say.

For the first time that week—or maybe ever—they hear something true about God. They learn that God is communicative, loving, and responsive and has a will for their life. They hear that all of us live in a world that is passing away and that God invites us to do his will in this world and be a part of his world in the next.

It is a stunning moment filled with hope and promise. For many people in the pews, it could be the first time in a long time they will take the idea of God seriously.

They expect the preacher to be serious about what is said in the sermon, well prepared and practiced, and able to articulate the deep things of God with passion and conviction. They may disagree with what is said. Many will. They may not believe what the preacher believes. Few do. *But they want to know that the preacher believes it.*

THE PULPIT LEADS THE WORLD

In Melville's Moby Dick, there is an early chapter when Ishmael heads to church before they set sail. The small chapel is near the shipping yard, and the building and interior show off nautical images. Ishmael notices these things as he enters the church. He is a first-time visitor.

The pulpit resembled the prow of a ship. Like a member of the crew, the preacher climbed into it using a worsted rope ladder. When ensconced in it, he hauled the ladder up behind him, rung by rung, and stood in the pulpit, towering over the congregation. It is a moment Ishmael will never forget.

The pastor, Fr. Mapple, delivers a brilliant stand-alone sermon on obedience from the Book of Jonah. Then, as the preacher descends the rope ladder at the end of the sermon, Melville waxes on about the task and burden of preaching. I wish every preacher would read, mark, learn, and inwardly digest this amazing scene from Melville's classic.

I'll quote the author's words so every preacher can wrestle with its incredible claims.

> *What could be more full of meaning?—for the pulpit is ever this earth's foremost part; all the rest comes in its rear; the pulpit leads the world. From thence, the storm of God's quick wrath is first described, and the bow must bear the earliest brunt. From thence, the God of breezes, fair or foul, is first invoked for favorable winds. Yes, the world's a ship on its passage out and not a voyage complete, and the pulpit is its prow.*

MOBY DICK, CHAPTER 8

"The pulpit leads the world." These words have rung in my ears since I read them for a literature class as a Sophomore in college. Indeed, they have been a driving force and inspiration for my preaching over the following 40 years. The words speak to me of the preacher's clear task, especially in these days of confusion.

That may seem like an unfair burden on preachers. It might be. But I hope it can also encourage all preachers to be as serious about their sermons as they hope their congregation is when they listen.

CONCLUSION

Music touches hearts, preaching illuminates minds, friendships nourish souls, and accessible leadership builds trust. When we excel in these areas, we don't just attract visitors; we create a space where people can find God and discover a sense of belonging.

Visitors come with questions, hopes, and a desire to connect with something greater than themselves. They overcome barriers in their own lives to attend for the first time. But they are also drawn to the Lord's church. While visitors may have certain expectations, it is ultimately God who has stirred something in their hearts.

It should be a privilege and responsibility to honor this event— attending church— by providing a welcoming place where they can deeply explore the faith and also where it can be clearly explained.

As you read through the summary points below, take time to prayerfully consider how your church can become a place where visitors encounter the living God and find a spiritual home. Remember, church growth is not just about numbers but about creating a space where people can experience God's transformative love and grace.

REVIEW POINTS FOR DISCUSSION

- How can your church ensure that both music and preaching not only engage and inspire but also authentically reflect God's presence, meeting the spiritual hunger of visitors and regular attendees alike?
- Comment on this statement: *A worship service that is unrehearsed, led by people who are unprepared, using technology that is unreliable, will leave visitors underwhelmed and members understandably hesitant to invite others.*
- What can your church do to facilitate new and close friendship among people? How many members in the church would you call friends?
- How can church leaders make themselves more accessible to new visitors in a way that reflects Christ's love and openness, potentially deepening the visitor's connection to the church and to God?

SEVEN WAYS TO ENHANCE YOUR CHURCH'S WORSHIP

1. Implement a rigorous preparation process for all aspects of the service. This includes thorough rehearsals for music teams, comprehensive tech checks for sound, lighting, and visual elements, and ensuring all leaders are well-prepared for their roles. Regularly assess and upgrade your technology as needed. Train volunteers in their respective areas to maintain a high standard of quality. By consistently delivering polished, glitch-free services, you create an environment that both impresses visitors and instills confidence in members to invite others.

2. Implement a series to deepen the congregation's understanding of worship as a spiritual encounter. This series would help members and visitors alike appreciate how each element of worship can draw them closer to God.

3. Develop a strategic plan to invest in the spiritual growth of your preaching and music ministries. The Vestry should prioritize allocating resources for Continuing Education and spiritual development of these key ministry leaders each year.

4. Establish a team dedicated to nurturing the spiritual vitality of worship practices. This team would help keep the worship experience spiritually nourishing and relevant while maintaining theological integrity and addressing the "Is it true?" question visitors bring.

5. Implement quarterly "All-Church Worship and Prayer Gatherings" focused on creating space for deeper spiritual encounters. These special services would provide opportunities for more immersive experiences of God's presence and community prayer.

6. Develop a program to incorporate various expressions of God-given creativity in services. This program would enrich the worship experience by integrating diverse art forms like

dance, visual arts, or drama, reflecting the multifaceted nature of God's creation.

7. Invest in enhancing the quality and intentionality of fellowship time after services. This simple yet effective change can foster the kind of genuine community and friendship-building that visitors seek, creating opportunities for spiritual conversations and connections.

Write your thoughts, ideas, comments here:

_____
_____
_____
_____
_____
_____
_____
_____
_____
_____

THE FOURTH TOOL - TRAINING
EDUCATE AND EQUIP ACROSS ALL AGES

Almighty God, who has entrusted us with the nurture and care of your people: Grant that our churches may be places where children, youth, and adults alike can grow in the knowledge and love of you. Help us to value the unique roles and responsibilities of each generation, and give us wisdom as we seek to foster a culture of lifelong learning and discipleship. May our efforts bear fruit in lives transformed by your grace and truth through Jesus Christ our Lord, who lives and reigns with you and the Holy Spirit, one God, now and forever. Amen

As mentioned in the previous chapter, the findings regarding visitors' priorities are based on a 2016 Pew Research Study. It is a fascinating report that should be read thoroughly. But the report's headline says it all: *When searching for a new congregation, Americans value the quality of sermons and want to feel welcomed.* Then, the style of services (music) and location are next in line. Only 56% of the respondents were looking for children's programming.

Church leaders should be sensitive to what visitors and new members seek in a new church. However, worship is not a commodity to be shaped and sold to please customers. In other words, we should not let visitors set the church's agenda or priorities.

So, let's frame the question another way. Rather than asking what the visitor is looking for in a church, let's be bold enough to imagine answering a more provocative question: *What is the Lord looking for in a church?* From there, we can see the church's fourth tool to foster growth: adult teaching and training.

I want to offer a mild caution as I approach this topic. I became nervous as I wrote this chapter and included everything I wanted to say about children's, youth ministry, and adult education. I ask for the reader's patience and indulgence. Please read everything in this chapter and then form your opinion.

TRAINING ADULTS IN THEIR FAITH

Jesus had a special love and affection for children, as evidenced by the Synoptic Gospels.*He welcomed them, took them in his arms, and blessed them. These three accounts warrant congregations' development of robust, first-rate ministries for children.

However, we must not overlook that Jesus' primary focus in his earthly ministry was teaching and training adults. While recognizing the importance of young people, the church's core is its adults. Jesus cherished children, but he chose adults as his disciples. While the Gospels do not specifically show Jesus teaching children, they contain numerous accounts of him teaching adults.[†]

---

* The story of Jesus blessing the children occurs in Matthew 19:13-15; Mark 10:13-16; and Luke 18:15-17.

† I am grateful to my friend and colleague, the late Roberta Hestenes, for her ideas along these lines. An article in Christianity Today Bible Studies sums up her thinking. Well worth reading it here: https://www.christianitytoday.com/biblestudies/articles/churchhomeleadership/060118.html

Doesn't it seem that the modern church often emphasizes the reverse? We spend time, money, space, and volunteer hours primarily teaching children and much less time teaching and training adults to live as Christians in an unChristian world.

Stop for a moment and consider this: If you did not include the 20-25-minute sermon that adult church members hear on any given Sunday, how much time do members invest in learning the Christian faith or receiving training to live a Christian life?

Anytime I bring up this idea—that Jesus played with children and taught adults, while the modern Western church does the opposite, namely plays with adults and teaches children—I get stares from fellow and sometimes former friends!

However, please think of it this way: If adults in the church participate mainly in coffee hours, potlucks, or sports leagues, how will they grow as disciples of Christ? Without the training and teaching in the faith, they could well lack the knowledge and depth needed to lead their families and live out their faith in the adult world.

The Bible was primarily written for adults, addressing adult questions and problems. Adults shape society, whether positively or negatively. Adult Christians are called to be salt and light in a troubled world. Adults vote, work, and control the various institutions of society, including governments, schools, corporations, unions, social groups, charities, and churches.

However, many adult Christians do not know how to apply their intellect to a mature understanding of the Bible. They often assume that Scripture has little relevant or practical guidance for their real-world lives. To them, the Bible appears as a childhood relic rather than a living document with profound truths that require daily engagement and discernment.

The loving ministry of Jesus toward children should be enough to inspire church leaders to invest in new and younger generations of Christians. But my point is this: *that is not enough—not nearly enough.*

The adults in every congregation should be the focal point for well-thought-out, well-developed, theologically deep teaching and training programs and ministries. Every church should have intentional, Bible-based Christian education training and teaching programs for adults; otherwise, it is just whistling past the graveyard filled with dying churches.

THE ORIGINS AND IMPACT OF SUNDAY SCHOOL AND YOUTH MINISTRY

I want to be clear about the importance of Sunday School and Youth Ministry in a congregation. These ministries and programs are essential to modern church life and must be strengthened. But they did not always exist. As you will see from this very brief overview, they are relatively recent additions to church life, and their impact has been subject to the laws of unintended consequences.

Read now about the origin of each.

Sunday School

The Sunday school movement began in 18th-century Britain and was designed to provide basic education and moral instruction to children from poor and working-class families. Using the Bible as the primary textbook, the founders and early Sunday School teachers taught reading, writing, hygiene, manners, and Christian doctrine. Sunday schools spread to other countries and became the cornerstone of a church's ministry to children and their families.

The programs evolved to include a broader range of kids, activities, instructional methods, age-graded classrooms, and a standardized curriculum. This movement is likely to have significantly impacted the style and development of public school education in the next decades.

Sunday School gave countless children biblical knowledge and a Christian foundation. Thank the Lord for it. And thank the Lord for the countless men and women who have served as Sunday School teachers. And, of course, we can thank the Lord for Robert Raikes and Hannah More, the founders of the Sunday school movement, who were confirmed members of the Church of England. They were Anglicans!

However, did the Sunday school movement diminish parents' roles in their children's spiritual development? We can see how it might have. If we look at how families impart the Christian faith to their children today, there is often little to see. Many families have an osmosis approach to passing the faith to the next generation. Parents assume, *"Well, they will just pick it up from us."* Why? Because the illusion is set: if I send my kids to Sunday School at my church, they will learn to be Christians.

This is not a reasonable hope. Indeed, once we articulate it this way, we see its instant fallacy. Learning and living out the Christian faith takes far more training, teaching, and practice than the 26 hours each year of annual classroom instruction that most children get in Sunday school—if they have perfect attendance!

Youth Ministry

If the Sunday School program had these unintended consequences, so did Youth ministry. Although it had a different origin, it unwittingly had a similar impact. In the wake of World War II, American families grew increasingly concerned about the vulnerability of their children to totalitarian ideologies, having seen the alarming success of Nazi youth organizations like the Hitler Youth and the League of German Girls in indoctrinating young Germans.

These programs, including the Pioneer camps for boys aged 10 to 14, focused on physical fitness, outdoor skills, and ideological training, effectively grooming a generation of committed Nazis and future soldiers.

In response, the Youth for Christ movement emerged, led by evangelists such as Billy Graham, Torrey Johnson, and Bob Cook. Through mass rallies, radio broadcasts, literature, and music, they looked to reach young people with the gospel and provide them with a sense of belonging, identity, and purpose.

The movement's success inspired churches and parachurch organizations like Young Life, Campus Crusade for Christ, and InterVarsity Christian Fellowship to adopt similar strategies, creating separate programs and spaces for different age groups and employing contemporary music, media, and entertainment to attract and engage youth.

WHILE THESE TWO INITIATIVES—STAPLES IN EVERY CHURCH-- successfully captured and taught generations of children and young people, they also produced unintended consequences. By outsourcing their children's spiritual formation to church programs and specialized youth workers, parents inadvertently relinquished their vital role as primary teachers and mentors in their children's faith journey. As a result, the rise of youth ministry contributed to a generational disconnect and a compartmentalized approach to faith formation that continues to challenge the church today.

WHO CAN HANDLE THE TRUTH?

The world is grappling with important questions, and the prevailing ideologies of secular humanism and consumerism have failed to provide satisfying answers. This cultural void leaves people wandering, searching for truth and meaning. In this context, the church has a unique opportunity to step forward and offer the rich, substantive answers found within Christianity.

However, as this cultural moment presents itself, many congregations are ill-equipped to engage with these weighty matters. There is a wide gap between the world's hunger and a congregation's ability to serve solid food.

To address this, every congregation aspiring to build a generational church must reimagine itself as a training center for its adult members.

Rather than offering sporadic classes or occasional Bible studies, churches should develop comprehensive, structured, and in-depth approaches to adult spiritual and theological education. This might include courses in systematic theology, church history, intensive Bible study, practical ministry skills, and even biblical languages. The goal would be to equip every adult learner with the knowledge and tools to effectively engage with and respond to the secular worldview encountered daily.

How is adult teaching and training a tool for church growth and vitality? By offering a taste of the answers to important questions people are asking, a church can grow both in depth and in numbers.

Is this vision achievable in a local congregation? The answer largely depends on the commitment of senior leadership to lifelong learning, personal growth, and the development of their faith.

THE PASTOR AS LIFELONG LEARNER

Earlier, we noted Emerson's dictum that an institution is the lengthened shadow of a leader and that the Church should reflect the priorities and the heart of our Lord, the head of it.

But the saying is true on a micro-level, as well. The local congregation will reflect the senior leadership's investment in personal continuing education and spiritual growth. If the rector or senior pastor is a lifelong learner, diving deep into the Scriptures to learn greater things of God's nature, learning from and reading church history, listening to authorities from the past, and searching for more excellent ways to understand and apply biblical truth in the modern era—if all of this is true of the senior leadership, then Emerson's dictum still applies. The congregation will take on those interests and attributes as well.

In other words, the congregation will become the *"lengthened shadow"* of a pastor committed to lifelong learning and spiritual growth.

. . .

CONSIDER THE POINTS MADE IN THIS CHAPTER CAREFULLY. THEY ARE meant to be provocative and spur church leaders to address the need for more robust Adult Christian Education.

REVIEW POINTS FOR DISCUSSION

- How can churches balance investing in children's and youth ministries and prioritize adult education and discipleship?
- In what ways might parents be encouraged and equipped to take a more active role in their children's spiritual formation, working in partnership with the church?
- What steps can churches take to create engaging, relevant, and transformative adult education programs that help members apply biblical truths to their daily lives?
- How can churches foster a culture of lifelong learning and spiritual growth, recognizing that discipleship is an ongoing process beyond childhood and youth?\

SEVEN WAYS TO INCREASE TEACHING AND TRAINING

1. Develop a comprehensive pathway for all age groups. This pathway would provide clear next steps for spiritual growth, regardless of where an individual is in their faith journey.

2. Create a mentoring program pairing mature believers with newer Christians. This one-on-one approach allows for personalized guidance and support in spiritual growth.

3. Think of your congregation as a seminary. Establish regular short-term, focused studies on specific aspects of faith. These intensives would allow for deep dives into particular topics or spiritual disciplines.

4. Develop a resource to equip parents in discipling their children. This resource would help bridge the gap between the church and the home in spiritual formation.

5. Implement a program connecting spiritual growth with practical ministry. This program would help members apply their faith in tangible ways while serving others.

6. Establish a cohort for peer-to-peer accountability and encouragement. These groups would foster community and mutual support in the discipleship journey.

7. Everyone measures attendance in Sunday School for children. Start tracking how many adults are involved in teaching and training classes every week. We get more of what we pay attention to.

Write your thoughts, ideas, comments here:

_____

_____

_____

_____

_____

_____

_____

_____

_____

_____

THE FIFTH TOOL - SMALL GROUPS
DEVELOP AN ABUNDANCE OF FELLOWSHIP GROUPS

Gracious God, who has called us into fellowship with one another and with your Son, Jesus Christ: Grant that our churches may be places where every person can find a sense of belonging, purpose, and connection. Raise up faithful leaders who will guide and nurture small groups and help us embrace the transformative power of an authentic community. May our life together be a witness to the world of your boundless love and grace. We ask this through Jesus Christ our Lord, who lives and reigns with you and the Holy Spirit, one God, now and forever. Amen.

L et's ask a happy question: What if it works? What if our church grows?

It is not all that far-fetched. Amid the gloom and dire predictions of Christianity going extinct in the West, some recent reports of sudden surges in attendance at some churches in some cases.

There were definite reports of increasing attendance in England, where I first heard of the phenomenon. Then, I checked in with some in my own tribe, the Anglican Church in North America, and I heard the same things. (The article I wrote is in the Appendix.)

Here are a sample of some X messages:

> ...our average attendance is now higher than pre-Covid.

> ...our church increased from 149 to 201... and we meet in a cowshed barn. Seriously.

> We ran out of bulletins on Ash Wednesday (and that was Valentine's Day!), we're continually scrambling for more chairs to pull in, and we've had to prepare more Communion elements.

> We hit an all-time high on Easter Sunday at 285, but we've been consistently pretty high since Nov, with a big surge coming into Lent. More in my direct wheelhouse, our catechism classes have been roughly twice as large in the last 12 months; it's nearly all new families in the parish.

So, let's consider this happy question: What if church growth happens? Suppose the pastor is hard-working and preaches a few sermons a year about the compassionate heart of Jesus and how we can develop a heart for others.

As a result, the congregation's people remember and embrace the call of mission and Jesus's Great Commission. The congregation sees itself increasingly as an outpost for the Kingdom of God. Church members become eager to share the Gospel story and invite their neighbors and co-workers to attend. The church offers training classes to help people learn to share the Gospel with others in engaging and appealing ways.

Everything seems to be going very well.

The pastor brings a revised budget to the vestry or the church board to hire a staff assistant to keep track of visitors. It passes. They also approve an increase in the budget to spruce up the property and redo the signage around it. They approve a contract with a marketing company to increase their online presence.

Current members who use social media rush to join their church's Facebook page and begin to *Like* content—happily, these *Friends* forward the interesting content to their friends and followers.

Due to the addition of new staff, the processes for inviting, welcoming, receiving, and engaging new people are in place. Attendance has increased, visitors are more frequent, and new member classes are full. Plans are underway to start a new worship service on Sunday morning.

The church is suddenly surging! Last year, the average number of attendees each week was 200, but it's 40% more this year! Everyone is happy to see the newcomers. God is favoring the congregation. There are 80 more people in church every week than a year ago.

Again, here is the great question to ask: *What if it works and your church begins to grow?*

THE CRITICAL QUESTION

But here is an even more important question: *What will these new people do at their new church? How will they get involved?*

Worship is the key offering or program of the church. But we also know that if a new family does not '*plugin*' to a ministry program or a set of relationships in the church, they will likely fade away. How long do new people typically remain if they're uninvolved or unattached? It is hard to say, but visitor retention rates are never good, even at their best. Non-growing churches keep about 9% of their new visitors, and growing churches keep about 21%.*

---

* From "What Every Pastor Should Know" by Gary McIntosh & Charles Arn. Research indicated that non-growing churches retained approximately 9% of their first-time

But here is a problem. Most active church members, especially the staff and leadership board, believe there are ample opportunities to get plugged in somewhere. Often, churches have events like "Ministry Fairs" or "Volunteer Recruitment Drives" to help people commit to the congregation. Sometimes, people persuade the pastor to make guilt-laden requests for signups.

However, the reality for a newcomer is quite different. When they look at the established programs of the church, they often see what appears to be a fortress of existing relationships and experiences—a wall they can't overcome. This perception creates a significant barrier to involvement.

To complicate matters further, while the vestry and leadership team may see a full array of activities and many people involved, the reality is that a core group of individuals is often doing multiple things in the church. The same person might be the head of a committee, serve as an usher, care for the grounds once a month, and act as a greeter. This concentration of responsibilities among a few can inadvertently make it even more challenging for newcomers to find their place.

But stop for a moment. Let's not make something easy, hard. Let's look at the program options in most churches. There are exceptions, to be sure, but most churches have only four categories of places to be involved. Let's take a quick look at them.

FOUR AREAS FOR ENGAGEMENT

Newcomers can usually choose from only four distinct areas or initiatives to make a significant connection.

1. Organizational Infrastructure: New people can join the church's organizational infrastructure and activity groups. These include the Altar Guild, Lay Readers, Ushers, Missions, Set-up Groups, Choir and

---

guests, while growing churches retained about 21%. In simple terms, this means 1 out of 10 or 1 out of 5 guests, neither of which is particularly impressive.

Musicians, and Greeters. Sunday school teachers, youth group leaders, assistants, and workers are included here. Many churches use these groups as a catch basin for new members. But as everyone soon finds out, vacancies are sometimes limited. Once someone becomes an usher, they don't readily surrender that position.

2. Governance and Oversight: Some new people can join groups of people who serve on committees or task forces to do something in the organization. The Vestry may have a Finance or Personnel Committee where new people might serve. These groups are busy helping set policies, budgets, etc., but they are hardly the place for new members to begin.

3. Adult Bible Studies: As mentioned in the last chapter, Bible studies, training programs, and adult classes are another important part of the church. These are essential for the well-being of a congregation. Bible studies are an excellent way for many new members to join the church. They can help the new members grow in their faith, deepen their knowledge of Scripture, and make new friends in the church.

The late Dr. Roberta Hestenes, mentioned in the previous chapter's footnote, wrote in her well-reasoned article:

> *Without slighting the importance of children and young people, I've always felt that the heartbeat of the church is adults. Jesus loved children, but he did not call children as his disciples. He called adults. The Gospels do not give an example of Jesus teaching children, but we have many, many stories of Jesus teaching adults.*

However, adult education classes and programs have a few challenges. They require three things that are often in short supply in most churches:

- Space—usually, groups like this meet on campus.
- Teachers—educated laypeople or ordained ministers should teach or lead Bible studies.

- Options—the schedule when these classes are offered is often inconvenient for working people.

So again, let us ask the question: Where will new visitors and members connect to the church? Where will they be engaged? Some involvement can come from Bible studies, volunteer roles, and committee positions, but these often have limited capacity.

4. Small Fellowship Groups: Finally, the last category of church involvement is a small group program. Sometimes, they are known as life groups or regular fellowship groups. These groups help members grow in their faith, make new friends, and develop a sense of attachment to the congregation and its mission.

Small groups are the lifeblood of a thriving church. They usually meet in people's homes. (No campus space is usually required.) They are led or facilitated by committed lay people trained for the task. They are entirely scalable and often self-perpetuating. They need little or no staff support or supervision. And they provide a first line of pastoral care and connection to the small group members.

ORNAMENTS OR INSTRUMENTS

For 40 years, I have led and studied congregations. I have seen churches flourish and increase their ministries yearly, and other churches struggle to grow and support their ministries. I have been a preacher, teacher, and worshipper in small, large, and mid-size congregations on Sundays.

I can say this: A small group program that regularly involves church members in off-campus, lay-led, bible-focused groups meeting every two weeks is the key difference between a growing, thriving congregation and one struggling with traction and momentum.

I have never seen a church grow without a solid small-group program. Never. And I have never seen a church with a robust small-group fellowship ministry that was not growing.

Thriving churches do not add small groups as an afterthought or a last-ditch effort to assimilate people. Instead, small groups—whether called faith groups, life groups, or fellowship groups—are fundamental to the DNA of these congregations from the outset. They are not *ornaments* adorning the tree but vital *instruments* through which the church becomes a growing organism.

In every case of a growing church, I have noticed an ability to do something that other churches don't seem to know to do. *Growing churches know how to handle visitors, and they have a nearly friction-less way of helping visitors find a small group to join, belong to, or connect with.* Period.

CASE STUDY

My wife and I started Christ Church as a Small Group Fellowship in the Spring of 1985. Our approach was to delay any form of public worship as long as we could until we had at least 80 in small group meetings every week on a non-Sunday morning event. After three months of these core meetings, we opened our doors (in a rented school) to well over 240 people. We had a slight dip over the next few weeks, bottomed out at about 140 people, and then grew from there.

At that time, I did not understand the wisdom of this "put-it-off" approach, but I do now. We had people joining our church and expecting (and wanting) to be involved somewhere, but there was nothing going on. There was nothing to do—except Small Groups.

There were no programs needing volunteers, no committees that needed leadership, and no Bible studies because there was no place to meet. We had no space. For those early months, all we were were half-a-dozen small groups meeting around the city following a curriculum I had pre-selected.

From there, Christ Church grew as a (mainly) Small Group oriented church. Years later, as the congregation fell into a normal pattern of programs and activities, the small groups became less of our focus. I regret this because the groups brought benefits to the church, to the people, and to the body of Christ.

We will discuss the community aspects of a small group emphasis in the next chapter. But before moving on, please take a few minutes to consider these questions. Be sure to make your marginal notes in the book or a notebook.

REVIEW POINTS FOR DISCUSSION

- How can churches effectively communicate the importance of small groups and encourage new members to join one as a primary means of connection and engagement?
- How can church leaders ensure that small group leaders are well-trained, supported, and equipped?
- How can churches regularly assess the health and effectiveness of their small group ministry, making adjustments as needed to ensure that groups remain vibrant, welcoming, and transformative?

SEVEN WAYS TO BUILD SMALL GROUPS

1. Develop a diverse range of small groups that reflect different life stages, interests, and needs. This variety ensures that every member can find a group where they belong.

2. Implement a training program for small group leaders. This training equips leaders with the skills and knowledge to facilitate effective, transformative group experiences.

3. Create a "Small Group Connection" event to help members find the right group. This event would make it easier for individuals to explore options and connect with a group that fits their needs.

4. Establish a system to support and guide group leaders. These coaches would provide ongoing mentorship and resources to ensure the health and effectiveness of small groups.

5. Implement a strategy to foster growth and new leadership. This approach helps groups stay vibrant and creates opportunities for new leaders to emerge.

6. Create a "Virtual Small Group" option for those unable to attend in person. This option will increase accessibility and allow broader partic-ipation in the small group ministry.

7. Implement an initiative to foster outward focus and community impact. These projects help groups bond while also serving the wider community.

Write your thoughts, ideas, comments here:

_____

_____

_____

_____

_____

_____

_____

_____

_____

_____

THE SIXTH TOOL – COMMUNITY

BUILD AND NURTURE STRONG RELATIONSHIPS

Almighty God, who has called us to live in community and to bear one another's burdens: We give thanks for the gift of fellowship where we can grow in faith, love, and service. Grant us wisdom as we seek to create safe and nurturing environments for all, especially for the children and vulnerable among us. May our meetings and groups be places of transformation, where your love is shared and your Kingdom is made known. We ask this through Jesus Christ our Lord, who lives and reigns with you and the Holy Spirit, one God, now and forever. Amen.

I used only seven hand tools to build my cherrywood rocker, but in some cases, I used two tools at once. A chisel is useful here and there by itself, but most chisels require a solid mallet to give them a good whack to cut the wood.

Similarly, the tools of Small Groups and Community go hand in hand. It is easy to see that. Small Groups are essential to the life of a thriving church. Why? Because they are integral because many people can find what they are looking for in them. Indeed, something happens in most small groups that satisfies people's deep needs: Community.

DEEP FRIENDSHIPS

Consider the behind-the-scenes life of the early church. The immediate effect of the outpouring of the Holy Spirit of God, as recorded in the Book of Acts, was a deep, rich, interconnected fellowship of close friends empowered for mission. Right after the experience of Pentecost and Peter's marvelous sermon, the church started to grow.

Acts 2:42 is well-known as a description of the lifestyle and practices of the early Christians. But if we examine what happened after Pentecost, we have a more complete picture of what the early church was like.

Luke writes that the newly empowered Christians…

> *…devoted themselves to the apostles' teaching and the fellowship, to the breaking of bread and the prayers. And awe came upon every soul, and many wonders and signs were being done through the apostles. And all who believed were together and had all things in common. And they were selling their possessions and belongings and distributing the proceeds to all, as any had need. And day by day, attending the temple together and breaking bread in their homes, they received their food with glad and generous hearts, praising God and having favor with all the people. And the Lord added to their number day by day those who were being saved.*

ACTS 2:42-47

These were the activities of their new life: *learning from the Apostles, fellowship, sharing meals, praying, witnessing miracles, sharing possessions, selling belongings to help others, attending the temple, eating together in homes, praising God, and welcoming new believers into their growing community.*

Do you notice something about this list? All of these activities are done with others. As we saw earlier with the Apostle Paul, Christianity was not a solo sport. The Christian faith is not just a personal experience, a singular mindset, or an individual's philosophy of life. It is all those things, at least. But it is also a close connection between people who love the Lord and each other and serve the Lord and one another.

But let's underscore this point: if we survey the early church's life and read the epistles of Peter, Paul, and John, something stands out. They dealt with serious issues; there were doctrinal things to be clear about. But nearly every letter speaks to the reader at a heart level. There was an assumption of deep fellowship and friendships across the church body. There was an assumption of a community of people under the direction and leadership of the Risen Lord.

The friendships they enjoyed were not merely acquaintances. They were partners in the Lord. There was a common unity among them. They were a community.

I mentioned that Small Groups are the sign of a growing church; they cause it. The reason for this is not rocket science. Don't make easy, hard. Churches with small groups grow because they provide something that everyone wants, few people have, and everyone who has it knows how special it is. Small groups foster a sense of community.

$1000 INVESTMENT PAYS OUT

As the founding rector of Christ Church in Plano, Texas, in 1985, I witnessed its growth into a large congregation for various reasons. However, a single purchase I made within the first month facilitated growth year after year: a professional engraving machine. I recruited a volunteer to make nametags for everyone. The cost for the machine was just under $1,000—a considerable expense in 1985.

It's an old-school idea, and many modern church planters and leaders are allergic to it. But consider what a simple nametag machine accomplished:

- It gave members a tangible sign of their membership in our new church.
- It allowed everyone to be known by others.
- It created a sense of community by eliminating the need to guess names or feel embarrassed when forgetting them.

When defending my purchase to the Vestry at our next meeting, I used this talking point: *I don't want anyone in this church to seem invisible, unknown, or disconnected from this church family.*

In essence, I wanted everyone to have every opportunity to know others and be known by name. This is the impact that small groups can have on our congregations. Everyone who participates in one will know others and be known by name.

STRUCTURED SMALL GROUPS ARE NOT THE ONLY WAY TO HELP PEOPLE experience community. Other kinds of groups build similar bonds of fellowship. Let's mention only a few types of groups.

FAITH GROUPS

Missions Groups and Prayer Groups are two distinct types of small groups that serve a similar function: they provide opportunities for members to exercise their faith actively and grow deeper in their understanding of the Gospel and the power of the Holy Spirit.

Missions Groups focus on preparing for and participating in outreach experiences. Members meet regularly to pray, study the Bible, fundraise, and encourage one another as they prepare for mission trips. During these trips, they work together outside their comfort zones, sharing the Gospel, serving others, and witnessing God's work firsthand. The intense shared experiences often result in tight-knit bonds and lifelong friendships. Upon returning, they continue to meet, debriefing and sharing stories of God's faithfulness, further deepening their faith and sense of community.

On the other hand, prayer groups meet regularly to intercede for the needs and concerns of others within the church and community. These groups provide a space for members to exercise their gift of intercession, comfort one another, and witness the power of prayer in action. They develop an intimate knowledge of the struggles and joys within their church family, often serving as a vital resource for pastors in times of crisis or celebration. Through their consistent practice of prayer and the experience of seeing God's responses, members grow in their faith and form deep, lasting connections with one another.

Both groups offer unique but equally powerful ways for church members to actively engage with their faith, experience the work of the Holy Spirit, and form meaningful relationships within the church community.

FOYER GROUPS

As a young boy, I remember the rector of our church making announcements about a third kind of group: a Foyer Group. It was prevalent back in the day, and because of its simplicity and flexibility, it has every reason to make a comeback.

Foyer Groups* are rooted in the Anglican tradition. They offer a unique and immediate way to foster community, sharing, conversation, and fellowship. Originating from the Cathedral of St. Michael in Coventry, England, during the aftermath of World War II, these groups embodied the spirit of reconciliation and understanding. Named after the French word for "hearth," Foyer Groups create a warm, inviting atmosphere

---

* Google the term "Foyer Group" to read about their rich history. One church I know calls these kinds of groups "Nine to Dine," which allows people to know that they are not just for married couples.

where adults can gather informally, yet regularly, to share meals and experiences.

At their core, Foyer Groups are designed to bridge the subtle divisions that often separate people within a congregation. By meeting in homes and sharing meals, these groups provide a relaxed setting for meaningful conversations and exchanging ideas, experiences, and even common problems. This informal approach allows deeper connections to form naturally, fostering a sense of belonging and community beyond the church walls.

The Apostle Paul was deeply serious about sharing the faith and spreading the Good News of Jesus Christ. But it was not all work, all the time. He admits, rather offhandedly, that he would love some 'down time' with people in the church. He wrote the Romans, whom he had not met yet, of his hope to be together *"that you and I may be mutually encouraged by each other's faith."* (Romans 1:12)

It would be appropriate to conclude each evening in the Foyer Group Format with a directed service of Compline from the Book of Common Prayer.

THE DELICATE BALANCE OF COMMUNITY

Community is not a natural phenomenon in our increasingly individualistic society. It is rare and precious, requiring intentional effort to cultivate and maintain. However, leaders must understand that while community can be fostered, it cannot be forced. An authentic community may begin spontaneously but won't endure without careful nurturing.

The church leadership should create an environment where a community can flourish while ensuring it remains safe for all participants. This involves setting clear expectations, modeling healthy relationships, and protecting the vulnerable. Remember, a true community is built on trust, which takes time to develop.

The leadership can transform the congregation's approach to the community if they see the church as a sort of Friendship Factory. Everyone, from the pastor to the newest member, should actively seek opportunities for connection. A few practical steps can make a significant difference:

- Improving the coffee and lengthening the time to enjoy it says to everyone: Stay around. Meet! Greet! Talk!
- Implementing a greeter rotation program involving different families or individuals each week ensures that visitors are warmly welcomed and introduces them to other church members.
- Food is a great socializer and essential for Christian fellowship. Hosting monthly or quarterly Newcomer Lunches could be extraordinarily effective.
- Establishing a dedicated Welcome Team that follows up with visitors through phone calls, emails, or home visits within a week of their first visit demonstrates genuine care and interest in integrating newcomers into the church family.

The church is not just a place of worship but a true community where people feel known, loved, and supported. In this environment of intentional friendship-building, faith flourishes, discipleship deepens, and the church becomes a powerful witness to the transformative love of Christ.

LIABILITIES AND YOU

We've explored the many benefits of small groups and the church as a community. However, as we foster deep connections and community, we must also be vigilant in protecting the vulnerable members of our congregation, particularly children.*

---

* The church should always protect its youngest members. Additionally, churches should not take on undue liability which might threaten their mission. State laws may

Prioritizing the protection of children, honoring marriages, and maintaining appropriate boundaries within a church is crucial for fostering a healthy, trust-filled environment. Many have experienced the pain of betrayal or boundary violations, and we must be mindful of their healing journey.

Let's remain vigilant. While community is essential to our faith, we must also recognize that, like all precious gifts, it requires careful stewardship to ensure it remains a source of support and growth rather than an opportunity for misuse. By nurturing a culture of respect, transparency, and accountability, we can create a thriving, safe space for all members to flourish in their faith journey.

Ignoring the need to protect children, respect marriages, and avoid even the appearance of improper relationships in the body of Christ is foolish and, in the end, could be cruel. Whenever these terrible things come to light—and they always do and as they always must—it has a cancerous effect on the rest of the community.

Be advised. Community is essential. But like all important things of God, the Enemy can use and abuse it for ugly purposes.

REMEMBER, COMMUNITY IS NOT JUST A NICE-TO-HAVE; IT'S ESSENTIAL for church growth and spiritual development. As a leader, your role in fostering this community is crucial.

But first, consider some of the ideas in this chapter as they apply to your congregation.

REVIEW POINTS FOR DISCUSSION

1. How well does our church offer ministry opportunities for

---

vary, and good counsel is available on various sites. This site was particularly helpful: https://www.simmsshowerslaw.com/protecting-children-in-church-small-group-settings/

members to develop deep, lasting friendships? How are we a Friendship Factory?

2. How can church leaders effectively communicate the vital role of small groups and inspire our members to participate?

3. How can we consistently evaluate and improve their small group ecosystems?

4. How can our church balance providing structure and support for small groups and allowing room for organic growth, creativity, and adaptation to each group's unique needs?

SEVEN WAYS TO BUILD COMMUNITY

1. Create a program to connect newer members with established ones. This program facilitates intentional relationship-building and helps integrate new members into the church community.

2. Develop a series throughout the year (game nights, potlucks, outings). These events provide casual settings for relationships to form and deepen.

3. Establish groups based on shared interests or life stages to foster natural friendships. These groups allow people to connect over everyday experiences or hobbies.

4. Implement a Greeting Time after services that encourage meaningful interactions. This structured time helps break the ice and facilitates connections beyond superficial hellos.

5. Develop a workshop series teaching communication, conflict resolution, and empathy. These workshops equip members with tools to build and maintain healthy relationships.

6. Implement a process to ensure newcomers quickly form connections. This process helps prevent new members from falling through the cracks and feeling isolated.

7. Where do name tags belong in your church? Can members learn and remember each other's names? This simple practice can significantly lower barriers to initiating conversations and building relationships.

Write your thoughts, ideas, comments here:

_____

_____

_____

_____

_____

_____

_____

_____

_____

_____

THE SEVENTH TOOL – PLANNING

SEE AND SHAPE THE FUTURE TOGETHER

Almighty God, who has called us to foster both spiritual growth and organizational wisdom: Grant us the grace to diligently engage in the work of planning and leadership. Endow our church leaders with vision and discernment as they cultivate the spiritual soil and chart the course for our community's future. May our strategic efforts be Spirit-led, combining the mystery of Your divine work with the method of our human endeavor. This we ask through Jesus Christ our Lord, who lives and reigns with You and the Holy Spirit, one God, now and forever. Amen.

Woodworkers use a measuring device to lay out a plan for furniture—sometimes a tape measure. If they build copies of furniture, they use a "storystick." A storystick is not a tool, per se; it is a piece of wood with all the marks and measurements from previous builds.

In many ways, a church's history is like a storystick. It carries the marks of its journey, the measurements of its growth, and the wisdom gained from past experiences. Just as a woodworker uses a storystick to replicate successful designs, church leaders can use their church's storystick to guide future growth and development.

But how does a church begin? Where does it come from? How did it start?

Some readers of this book will remember the days when they were part of their church planting team—they were part of the start-up. Other readers were not involved in the early stages of their congregation. They joined the church years after the so-called early days.

Regardless of when you joined, it's good to remember or at least imagine what happened in the beginning. Understanding the church's origins helps us appreciate the marks on our spiritual storystick and guides us in adding new ones.

The Apostle Paul, in his wisdom, gave us two powerful metaphors for understanding church growth: an agricultural image and an architectural image. These metaphors reveal two essential types of church leaders. Some are one kind, and some are the other. But in most cases, the startup leader must be both. They must understand and embody their role as a planter and a planner.

Look closely at this well-known passage from the Apostle:

> I planted, Apollos watered, but God gave the growth. So neither he who plants nor he who waters is anything, but only God who gives the growth. He who plants and he who waters are one, and each will receive his wages according to his labor. For we are God's fellow workers. You are God's field, God's building.
>
> According to the grace of God given to me, like a skilled master builder I laid a foundation, and someone else is building upon it. Let each one take care how he builds upon it.

1 CORINTHIANS 3:6-9

THE PLANTER

When discussing the start of new churches, we often use Paul's agricultural metaphor, referring to them as "plants" and their founders as "planters." This imagery acknowledges that God brings growth, and the planter's role is to cultivate and protect the fledgling congregation.

I was a church planter. I loved telling people of the work I was doing. I was planting a church. The phrase lent an 'old earth' quality to the effort. It seemed rugged and sweaty.

"Planting a church" implies a mystery and miracle to the effort. A farmer plants a seed or a shoot and prepares the soil with fertilizer, turning it over and over. Then, the farmer adds the water and protects the seedlings from crows or varmints. And he waits. And he waits some more.

That is the mystery. By God's grace, the seed will germinate, sprout roots, and grow. Is there anything a planter can do besides prepare the soil, diligently water, and wait? Yes-pray!

This diligence in preparation is necessary when planting a church and leading an established congregation. The pastor as a farmer is a very apt, accurate description.

THE PLANNER

However, if we follow the Apostle Paul's thinking, there is more to do. There is another kind of activity besides planting and waiting. We must plan and build!

Do not overlook the other metaphor Paul uses to describe starting a church. It is a concept from the world of architecture and engineering, and it is just as powerful as the agricultural image. Just as a church starter is a "planter," he should also be a master builder or a planner. In Greek, the word used is *"arch-craftsman!"*

Paul writes, *"Like a skilled master builder, I laid a foundation, and someone else is building upon it."* It is not an overstatement to say that a church leader should be both a planter and a planner. Another way to make the same point is to say this: church leadership is both farming (planting) and framing (planning).

The *planter* prepares the soil, tears out weeds, tills the soil, waters regularly, chases away pests, fertilizes the ground, and waits for rain, sunshine, and the proper temperatures. They are a farmer. The *planner* thinks ahead, develops leaders, assigns tasks, teaches basics, thinks through processes, coordinates supplies, and decides on logistics and delegation. They are a framer.

Both roles are crucial in creating a church's storystick—a legacy of growth, wisdom, and faith that can guide future generations. The planter's marks on the storystick might represent moments of miraculous growth or seasons of patient waiting. The planner's marks might indicate strategic decisions, structural improvements, or visionary goals achieved.

PLANNING: ADDING MARKS TO THE STORYSTICK

Winston Churchill said, *"Plans are of little importance, but planning is essential."* We know what he means, even if it is overstated a bit. He means that the process of planning is crucial. Planning allows you to think through possibilities, prepare for contingencies, and adapt and change if circumstances change. In essence, planning is how we intentionally add marks to our church's storystick.

Few preachers enter the pulpit unprepared, waiting and hoping for the power of the Holy Spirit to speak through them. Every preacher takes the time and makes an effort to, as the Anglican collect says, *"read, mark, learn, and inwardly digest"* the Scriptures. Then, the preacher plans what to say, how it should be said, and in what order. Then, in the pulpit, God the Holy Spirit has something to work with!

The same is true for church leadership. Leaders who lead must be leaders who plan. Each plan becomes a potential mark on our storystick, guiding future growth and development.

Planning in the church context is a prayerful and intentional process by which the rector or lead pastor, as both planter and planner, discerns God's vision for the congregation and maps out the practical steps to realize that vision.

The process combines the organic, Spirit-led approach of a farmer nurturing crops with the structured, forward-thinking mindset of an architect designing a building. These combined approaches create a rich and nuanced storystick that reflects the mystery of God's work and the method of human effort.

PLANNING ANSWERS TWO QUESTIONS

For many years, I have advocated that church leaders must get away—sometimes far away—from the daily duties of ministry and prayerfully enter into what I call a 'dreaming stage.' Without getting too mystical about it, I have used the language of 'dreaming' to describe this process:

God has a dream for his people, a preferred future, and a plan to achieve it. It is his will. And because God has a dream, he looks for a dreamer who will dare to prayerfully ask what He wants from me to accomplish what He wants for His people.

Leaders need to be dreamers. They must see into the future with faith and imagine what could be done for the best interests of God's people and the glory of His Name. These dreams and visions become the most significant marks on our storystick, guiding the overall direction of our church's growth.

Leaders then need to write that down. They should be as specific as possible with the details of the dream. The leader should know that they will need the input and support of others to develop the vision, but the designated dreamer should provide the first description of it.

We see this in the Bible when Moses shares the dream (God's dream) of the Promised Land. He describes it to the people in vivid detail, painting a picture of the good things that await them. This vision becomes a powerful mark on Israel's storystick, guiding and motivating them through their journey.

> *For the Lord your God is bringing you into a good land, a land of brooks of water, of fountains and springs, flowing out in the valleys and hills, a land of wheat and barley, of vines and fig trees and pomegranates, a land of olive trees and honey, a land in which you will eat bread without scarcity, in which you will lack nothing, a land whose stones are iron, and out of whose hills you can dig copper. And you shall eat and be full, and you shall bless the Lord your God for the good land he has given you.*

DEUTERONOMY 8:7-10

When you read this, it is hard to argue with Moses. He is being precise and clear. He is giving his people hope. He is showing them the promise of the Promised Land. He is motivating them to stay the course. He is being the lead pastor of the flock.

Do you see how Moses describes his vision/dream with as much specificity as possible? He is answering the two questions that are on everyone's mind:

Where are we going? What will it be like for me and my family when we get there?

My point is that every church is filled with people who have the same two questions in their minds and hearts. And it is incumbent upon the leader to provide the answers. These answers become crucial marks on our church's storystick, helping to guide and reassure our congregation as we grow and change.

That is what planning is for. There is no way to arrive at the answers to these two questions other than to think and plan, dream and pray, take counsel and be still before the Lord in humility, and ask for the dream and the direction. As the subtitle to this chapter says, this is how the congregation can "see and shape the future together."

THE LEADER AND THE TEAM

Only one person can initiate this work of creating and marking our church's storystick. Only one. In the Anglican tradition, we have a vestry. Other denominations have boards or teams. These are the men and women who bring essential counsel, thoughts, refinements, challenges, and wisdom to the process and the plan—to the dream. But there is only one person who can kickstart this work—the appointed leader. In the Anglican tradition, this is the role of the rector of the parish—the designated dreamer.

While the leader holds this unique position, the success of planning and its implementation relies heavily on a team approach. The elected leadership body brings diverse perspectives and skills to the table. Staff members provide invaluable insights into the practical aspects of implementing the vision. They often serve as the bridge between the high-level strategic plan and the ground-level execution.

Together, the "leader/board/staff" team put marks on the storystick to ensure that the church's growth aligns with the shared vision and values. Together, they see and shape the future.

When approached as a collaborative, Spirit-led process, strategic planning becomes a powerful tool for church growth and vitality. It combines the mystery of God's work (planting and waiting) with the method of human effort (planning and working). Planning recognizes the church's dual nature: a living, organic community and a structured organization requiring purposeful guidance.

. . .

WE ARE NEAR THE END OF THIS SHORT BOOK ON THE TOOLS THAT EVERY church has to cultivate church growth and facilitate congregations. After each chapter, I invited you to add your thoughts and ideas as an ordained or lay leader in your congregation.

REVIEW POINTS FOR DISCUSSION

1. How does the concept of a *storystick* apply to your church's history and future planning? Discuss some significant "marks" on your church's storystick and how they have shaped your congregation.

2. Reflect on the dual roles of "planter" and "planner" in church leadership. How do these roles manifest in your church's current leadership, and how might they be balanced more effectively?

3. Consider the two key questions Moses answered for his people: "Where are we going?" and "What will it be like for me and my family?" How well does your church's leadership address these questions for your congregation? What could be improved?

4. Discuss the process of "dreaming" or visioning for your church. How does your leadership team currently approach strategic planning? How might you incorporate more intentional "dreaming" into this process?

SEVEN WAYS TO INCREASE EFFECTIVE PLANNING

1. Establish an annual Strategic Planning Retreat for church leadership. This retreat provides focused time for vision-casting, goal-setting, and strategic thinking.

2. Implement a Vision Team responsible for long-term planning and goal-setting. This team ensures the church maintains a forward-looking perspective and plans for future growth and challenges.

3. Develop a Ministry Evaluation process to regularly assess the effectiveness of church programs. This process helps ensure that church activities remain aligned with the overall vision and are producing desired outcomes.

4. Create a Strategic Communication Plan to keep the congregation informed and engaged with the church's vision. This plan helps maintain transparency and fosters buy-in from the congregation.

5. Implement a review to ensure finances and volunteers are aligned with strategic priorities. This review helps maximize the impact of the church's resources in achieving its mission.

6. Establish a process to inform outreach strategies. This assessment helps the church remain relevant and responsive to the actual needs of its surrounding community.

7. Implement an effort that aligns prayer with the church's strategic goals. This initiative spiritually undergirds the church's plans. It reminds everyone of the ultimate source of the church's vision and growth.

Write your thoughts, ideas, comments here:

_____

_____

_____

_____

_____

_____

_____

_____

_____

_____

CONCLUSION

As we conclude this book outlining the seven vital tools you already have, remember that together, they can be used to renew and revitalize your congregation. Here is what I mean:

1. By cultivating compassion and developing empathy for others, you lay the foundation for a caring community.
2. By focusing your efforts on aligning with your church's mission, you ensure that every action serves a higher purpose.
3. People in your community and around your church are drawn to worship services that will inspire them and exalt the name of our Lord.
4. As you build programs to train adults and invest in training that educates across all generations, you strengthen the membership to be disciples in the real world.
5. Small group opportunities help people easily connect with each other and form new friendships.
6. Your efforts to become a place where everyone knows someone—a community—make your church feel like a church home.
7. Finally, as you see and shape the future together through strategic planning, the God-given dreams of the leader and the people become reality.

These tools are not just theories—they are practical, powerful instruments of transformation. The work ahead may be challenging, but it is undoubtedly vital.

We must remember that all our efforts – whether in small groups, worship, training, or strategic planning – ultimately depend on God's grace and the work of the Holy Spirit. As Paul reminded the Corinthians, we may plant and water, but God gives the growth. And as we grow, may we continue to add meaningful marks to our church's story-stick, creating a legacy that will guide and inspire future generations.

ADDITIONAL RESOURCES

THE SEVEN TOOLS FOR SMALL CONGREGATIONS
THOUGHTS TO HELP THE SMALLER SIZE CONGREGATION

One of the early readers of this book commented that it had some excellent ideas and suggestions, but it was geared toward a middle to large church. What about the small congregation, he asked. This is a fair concern.

Allow me to make a few comments directed at the pastors and leaders of small churches about how The Seven Tools can be used.

NO SHAME

There is no shame in being a small church.

The early church was small and intimate. While we often hear about the thousands who came to believe in the Lord at the feast of Pentecost, it's important to remember that the churches founded by Paul on his missionary journeys were typically small, close-knit communities.

The churches in Corinth and Ephesus, which we often view as significant centers of early Christianity, likely had no more than 40-50 members each during Paul's time. In his book, The First Urban Christian, Wayne Meeks surprises us with an estimate of the size of the congregations and the total number of Christians in the well-known cities. *The total number of Christians in a city like Corinth or Ephesus during Paul's time may have been in the range of forty to one hundred individuals, including children.* *

These small gatherings were the backbone of the early Christian movement, fostering deep relationships, mutual support, and a passionate faith that would take over the Roman world.

Healthy and faithful small churches stand in this noble tradition, carrying forward the intimacy and community-focused nature of those early assemblies.

ASK FOUR QUESTIONS

While there is no shame in being small, it is not a virtue. There are often reasons why churches remain small, even if the community around them is growing. Size, no matter how large or small, is a neutral measurement. Every church—small churches included—should ask four questions to ensure they are seeing clearly.

1. Are we genuinely welcoming and integrating newcomers, or do we unintentionally create barriers that make it difficult for new people to feel at home?
2. Have we become too inward-focused, neglecting to engage with and serve our surrounding community?
3. Are we adapting our methods and approaches to effectively reach and connect with our area's changing demographics and needs?

---

* The First Urban Christians: The Social World of the Apostle Paul", Yale University Press, 2003, pg. 109.

4. Are we intentionally developing new leaders and empowering members to use their gifts, or are we overly reliant on a small core group?

These questions address common issues that might cause a church to remain small even in a growing community, such as lack of hospitality, insularity, resistance to change, and limited leadership development. They encourage self-reflection and can help identify potential blind spots in a church's approach to growth and community engagement.

USE YOUR SUPER POWER

While the ideas presented in "The Seven Tools" can benefit churches of all sizes, smaller congregations may need to adapt these concepts to fit their specific contexts. The key is to start small, prioritize efforts, and leverage your community's close-knit nature.

Don't be discouraged if you can't immediately implement every suggestion or concept. Instead, focus on quality over quantity, adapt ideas to your scale, and celebrate each step of progress.

Remember, in a smaller church, personal connections are your superpower. As you explore the seven tools – Compassion, Focus, Worship, Training, Small Groups, Community, and Planning – consider how each can be tailored to your church's unique situation and needs.

1. Start Small: Don't try to implement everything at once. Choose one or two areas to focus on initially.

2. Adapt to Your Context: Feel free to modify these ideas to fit your unique situation. What works in one church may need adjustment in another.

3. Leverage Your Strengths: Small churches often have stronger relationships, more flexibility, and a greater sense of ownership among members. Use these to your advantage.

4. Be Patient: Growth and change take time. Celebrate small victories and keep moving forward.

5. Engage Everyone: Everyone's contribution is significant in a small church. Find ways to involve each member in implementing these tools.

6. Stay Mission-Focused: Keep your church's mission and vision at the forefront. Let these guide your implementation of the seven tools.

7. Pray Continuously: Undergird all your efforts with prayer, seeking God's guidance and blessing on your church.

CONCLUSION

Small churches have played a vital role in Christianity from its earliest days, and they continue to be powerhouses of faith, community, and mission today.

Remember, it's not about competing with larger churches or trying to be something you're not. It's about faithfully stewarding the resources God has given you and creating a vibrant, Christ-centered community where people can grow in faith and service.

COME. SEE. GO. TELL.

A PROGRAM TEMPLATE FOR THE CONGREGATION USING THE SEVEN TOOLS

One of the most common situations I encounter while coaching pastors is one I faced in my parish ministry. I knew what I wanted to do and where I felt the Lord was leading our church. I had an idea of the outcome and could think of several steps to take to get there. But what was the next step? One pastor recently expressed this in a memorable way: "I have the picture, but I do not have a plan, at least a plan that matches our reality."

In other words, I knew what I needed to do; I didn't know what to do *next*.

As I wrote this book, I had several different kinds of churches in mind. I led my congregation for over 30 years and learned so much from that wonderful community of faith. Since leaving that role, I have served as a coach to many ordained leaders. Through this work, I've become acquainted with perhaps another 15-20 congregations. I had all of these churches in mind as I wrote this book.

COME. SEE. GO. TELL.

With those churches in mind and using all seven tools mentioned in this book, I have devised a template for any church to adapt or adopt. In this short chapter, I will lay out a way to guide the pastor, their staff, and the vestry/board into a season of growth and vitality. The plan I developed would take place over the next two years.

For the sake of explanation, I am calling the plan: ***Come. See. Go. Tell.*** The program's name is based on the angel's comments to the disciples at the end of Matthew's Gospel.

This statement is the big picture idea of what your church could accomplish over the next few years:

Become a compassionate church with a clear mission that creates inspiring worship, trains devoted followers of Christ across generations, cultivates deep fellowship through small groups and strong community, and proactively shapes its future through effective leadership and planning.

How could your church do this? Note the four steps below and on the following pages:

1. Take Measurements
2. Find Momentum
3. Build Muscle
4. Multiply and Deploy Membership

STEP ONE: TAKE MEASUREMENTS (TWO MONTHS)

- **Inform** the congregation about the leadership's commitment and prayers for church growth.
- **Baseline Data Collection:** Record current metrics, including: Overall attendance, Visitor numbers, Task and service groups, with volunteer counts, On-campus Bible studies, Home-based small groups, Prayer groups
- **Growth-Focused Prayers:** Develop a specific Collect for liturgical use and additional prayers to be incorporated into regular worship services.
- **Membership Pathway:** Create a clear, structured process to guide visitors in understanding church life and finding ways to engage.
- **Invitation Tool:** Design and produce invitation cards for members to use when inviting friends, neighbors, and coworkers.
- **Facility Preparation:** Thoroughly clean and improve the church's exterior, interior, and public spaces to enhance their appeal to visitors.
- **(Optional) Marketing Outreach:** Plan a marketing or social media campaign to increase community awareness and invite potential visitors.

This comprehensive two-month phase lays the groundwork for growth by involving the congregation, establishing benchmarks, enhancing spiritual focus, and preparing practical tools and spaces for welcoming new people.

STEP TWO: FIND MOMENTUM (FOUR MONTHS)

- **Compassion/Invitation Sermon Series:** Deliver a series of sermons focusing on the benefits of belief, designed to inspire members to share their faith and invite others.
- **Invitation Initiative:** Activate: Identify and encourage members willing to invite others. Train: Guide effective invitation methods. Equip: Supply necessary tools (e.g., invitation cards from Step One). Celebrate: Recognize and honor those who actively participate in inviting others.
- **Enhance Sunday Hospitality:** Form a dedicated Hospitality Team; Assign greeters for warm welcomes; Organize coffee service for a welcoming atmosphere; Implement an intake process for visitor information; Develop and execute a follow-up plan for visitors.
- **New Member Orientation:** Schedule and prepare for an orientation session to integrate new members into the church community.
- **Member Introduction:** Implement a regular practice of introducing and welcoming new members during services or church events.

This four-month phase focuses on creating a culture of invitation, improving the visitor experience, and integrating new members. It combines spiritual encouragement through sermons with practical steps to welcome and incorporate newcomers into the church community.

STEP THREE: BUILD MUSCLE (ONGOING)

- **Begin Small Group Program:** Implement a concentrated 3-month program for 12 Sundays.
- **Start Same-Gender Bible Studies:** Establish separate studies for men and women. Utilize video-driven formats for consistency and ease of facilitation.
- **Offer Foyer Dinner Groups:** Organize small, rotating dinner groups in members' homes; Conclude each gathering with Compline (evening prayer service)
- **Children's Ministry Enhancement:** Develop and promote engaging programs for children and youth; Focus on age-appropriate spiritual education and activities.

This six-month phase aims to deepen spiritual growth and community connections within the church. It provides structured opportunities for adults to engage in focused study and fellowship while strengthening the children's ministry.

Don't try to do everything at once. All three are possible, but only after the successful development of each one. The context of the local church will determine which one should come first. Simultaneously, the ongoing emphasis on children's ministry ensures that the church nurtures its youngest members and attracts families.

STEP FOUR: MULTIPLY AND DEPLOY MEMBERSHIP

- **Community Service Initiative:** Organize regular volunteer opportunities in the local community; Partner with local charities or start a church-led project; Encourage both new and long-time members to participate together
- **Leadership Development Track:** Identify potential leaders within the congregation; Provide a structured program for spiritual and practical leadership training; Gradually integrate participants into church leadership roles
- **Family Ministry Expansion:** Develop programs that engage entire families together; Offer parenting classes and support groups; Host regular family fun nights or weekend retreats; Create multi-generational worship experiences

These activities build upon the foundation laid in earlier phases by deepening engagement, fostering relationships across demographics, developing new leaders, and strengthening family units within the church community. They also provide fresh opportunities for new and existing members to become more involved in church life.

CONCLUSION

This template is not a one-size-fits-all solution. It is a roadmap that allows you to adapt to your unique context and congregation. The key is to start and maintain momentum.

Perhaps you'll implement all of these suggestions or cherry-pick the ideas that resonate most with your church's vision and needs. The important thing is to take action. Start with one or two initiatives from each phase that excite you and align with your church's strengths.

Remember, sustainable growth is gradual and intentional. Implementing even a portion of these suggestions leads your church toward greater vitality and impact. As you progress, you'll likely discover new ideas and opportunities specific to your community.

So, take heart and take action. Your journey towards a growing, thriving church begins with a single step. Which of these ideas will you implement first? The future of your church's growth and impact starts now.

May God bless your efforts as you faithfully lead your congregation into this new season of growth and renewal.

AN OPEN LETTER TO THE ANGLICAN CHURCH IN NORTH AMERICA

FROM DAVID ROSEBERRY

W hile I wrote this book for a congregation of any denomination, I want to address the brothers and sisters of the Anglican Church in North America and the bishops, clergy, and laity, my colleagues in the Lord.

We have faced many battles and paid significant costs to establish the ACNA. Now, we face a clear challenge: growing our congregations and fulfilling our mission as Christ's church in North America.

The seven tools discussed—Compassion, Focus, Worship, Training, Small Groups, Community, and Planning—are not just theoretical concepts. They are practical instruments that can transform our parishes and the entire Province. As I've shared with our newly elected archbishop, I believe our focus for the years ahead should be empowering our clergy and equipping our congregations across the Province.

I urge all ACNA leaders—from the College of Bishops to the diocesan leaders to individual parish vestries—to rediscover, sharpen, and use these tools and principles.

Imagine what our churches could become if they actively developed compassionate hearts among their members, focused on their mission, offered inspiring worship, continuously trained adults and children, fostered vibrant small groups, built authentic communities, and strategically planned for the future.

Remember that *"the fundamental agency of mission in the Province is the local congregation."* This remarkable statement, found in the Constitution and Canons of our Province, is pure gold. It is a viable pathway forward because it puts every church and every future church plant in the center of a provincial strategy. Stronger congregations mean a stronger witness and greater service to the Lord and the Gospel in North America.

To realize this potential, we must be willing to invest our time, energy, and resources into growing our congregations in healthy, sustainable, and Christ-centered ways. *The Seven Tools* provide a way to facilitate this growth, and it's up to the leaders of each congregation to put the tools into practice. Your role is crucial in this journey.

May God bless and guide us all as we enter the next chapter of our journey together, remembering that our actions today shape the future of our congregations and the Anglican Church in North America.

In Christ,

David Roseberry

ARE WE LIVING IN A CHRISTIAN SPRING?

WILL MORE INTEREST IN CHRISTIANITY DRAW MORE PEOPLE TO YOUR CHURCH?

This book began as a series of blog posts I wrote in the Spring of 2024. I responded to several tweets and observations on the X social media platform. As I finished this series on Anglican Compass, I started to see other posts that told me I was not crazy. Attendance was surging, and many people came back to the Christian faith.

It seemed fitting to include my original thinking here.

A CHRISTIAN SPRING?

Are there signs of a Christian Spring? I am not a researcher. I am a pastor. I am not trained to look for evidence of movements or trends, but I am an amateur student of history, and I hope for the church in the long term. This confidence comes from Jesus, who said the gates of Hell will not prevail against (the church). Strangely enough, I also have hope for the church in the short term. Here's why.

After Easter in 2024, I picked up a thread of tweets from church leaders citing tremendous and unexpected growth in attendance in their congregations over the last few months. They were not commenting on Easter crowds but on Easter-*like* trends. They used phrases like "packed auditorium," "crowds," and "surging attendance." Sounds promising.

However, since these churches were not Anglican, I thought I'd better check in with some of the congregations in my tribe, The Anglican Church in North America. So, I asked the Anglican Xers (formerly known as Tweeters) about their congregations. I posted this question:

> I have heard bits and pieces of a growing trend in churches toward greater attendance. Objectively, did you see greater attendance than usual over Lent/Easter? Please provide serious answers.

Here are just a few of the responses.

> We moved into a new (rented) space on Palm Sunday that gives us room to grow and had our largest Easter in our short history. Overall, we are up ~ 15% in 2024 compared to 2023 and encouraged to be moving through a key developmental threshold.

> Ours was higher, to the point even that we had to add extra seating in the narthex.

> Yep. We've had a good surge, even from the start of the year. Coming primarily from younger people/families.

Others wrote:

> We have long since recovered from the pandemic shutdowns, and our average attendance is now higher than pre-Covid.

> Ours, Church of the Lamb, increased from 149 to 201... and we meet in a cowshed barn. Seriously.

> We ran out of bulletins on Ash Wednesday (and that was Valentine's Day!), we're continually scrambling for more chairs to pull in, and we've had to prepare more Communion elements. These are encouraging problems.

> We hit an all-time high on Easter Sunday at 285, but we've been consistently pretty high since Nov, with a big surge coming into Lent. More in my direct wheelhouse, our catechism classes have been roughly twice as large in the last 12 months; it's nearly all new families in the parish.

There were other reports like this.

So, is something going on? I know this is not a scientific survey. I also know it was Easter, when there usually is a boost in attendance. But the sense I had from others was there was more to it than just "Christeasters" stopping in.[*]

A SEARCH FOR TRUTH?

I recently read Justin Brierley's excellent book, *The Surprising Rebirth of Belief in God*. It was a thrilling page-turner! Here are a few quotes from the early part of the book to help you understand why the author believes there is a resurgence of belief in God.

> *What's attractive about the (Christian) faith is precisely its countercultural stance—the "weirdness" of believing and living as if Jesus really*

---

[*] I love all the people who attend worship only on Christmas and Easter, but they have been dubbed "Christeasters" by many church leaders, although it is meant to be a harmless term.

has risen from the dead and is calling those who follow him to live a different story to the world around them.

...as the influence of New Atheism has waned, a variety of secular thinkers have been stepping forward to ask new questions about the value of religion and where the West is heading in the absence of the Christian story.

(New converts) found themselves drawn towards a story that made sense of their deepest longings and desires.

In his book, Brierley reports his in-depth conversations with Tom Holland, Jordan Peterson, and Douglas Murray. Not all of them claim a Christian faith, but each can feel themselves warming to the idea.

Is this a trend or a blip?

A TENDER CONVERSION STORY

Further, many have read Ayaan Hirsi Ali's account of her conversion to Christianity. She is a Somali-born Dutch/American activist, writer, intellectual, and politician. She is now an outspoken critic of her former faith. She came to understand that Islam is fundamentally incompatible with Western democratic values, especially those upholding the rights of women.

This is part of her story in her own words. *

Yet, I would not be truthful if I attributed my embrace of Christianity solely to the realization that atheism is too weak and divisive a doctrine to fortify us against our menacing foes. I have also turned to Christianity because I ultimately found life without any spiritual solace unendurable—indeed, very nearly self-destructive. Atheism

---

* Her account is compelling and is widely available on the Internet. It was first carried on Unherd, an online magazine. https://unherd.com/2023/11/why-i-am-now-a-christian/

failed to answer a simple question: What is the meaning and purpose of life?

There are stories of other thought leaders opening their hearts to the truth of the Gospel. Why? Because people are discovering that God is pervasively real. He is everywhere. Nobel Prize-winning physicist Werner Heisenberg is said to have commented:[*]

> *The first gulp from the glass of natural sciences will turn you into an atheist, but at the bottom of the glass, God is waiting for you.*

In other words, many are recognizing the vital role that the Gospel plays in shaping our society. Thomas Aquinas, a 13th-century theologian, asserted that theology was the queen of science and profoundly influenced every other academic pursuit. *"All truth is God's truth,"* said Augustine (AD 350-430). These words convey confidence in God, truth, the Bible, science, and the ultimate alignment of all things under Him.

Ultimately, the search for beauty, truth, and meaning leads us back to the source of all knowledge: our Triune God. Many people worldwide seem to recognize that too much of the Western world—our culture, tradition, morality, values, and ethics—could be at risk of being lost.

WHAT SHALL WE DO?

Is it Springtime? Is the ice of secularism thawing out? I'd like to think

---

[*]   There is some dispute about whether he said this. But these words from his book are equally wonderful and they convey the same idea: *"In the history of science, ever since the famous trial of Galileo, it has repeatedly been claimed that scientific truth cannot be reconciled with the religious interpretation of the world. Although I am now convinced that scientific truth is unassailable in its own field, I have never found it possible to dismiss the content of religious thinking as simply part of an outmoded phase in the consciousness of mankind, a part we shall have to give up from now on. Thus in the course of my life I have repeatedly been compelled to ponder on the relationship of these two regions of thought, for I have never been able to doubt the reality of that to which they point."* From "Scientific and Religious Truth" (1974).

so. Who wouldn't? Is it a blip? Or a trend? And, like all Springtime weather, we may not know until we discover the truth in hindsight.

We cannot know. But we can be ready. In fact, we should be ready now —ready at all time to invite, welcome, engage, develop, and fully embrace people into the fellowship of our congregations. Always and at all times.

That is the least we can do to fulfill the Great Commission. The Gospel is not to be kept secret or hidden under a bushel. At the very least, churches should be intentional in their efforts to share the Gospel with others and encourage people to join in their fellowship and faith. This is basic evangelism. This is basic hospitality. In fact, if you study the development of the early church, hospitality and evangelism seemed one and the same.

Does anyone doubt that churches and church members must always diligently seek and save the lost? This skill and habit are too easily ignored, forgotten, and lost. As we will see in the coming chapters, it is the exercise of the spiritual gift—the old-school tool of hospitality.

Consider this quote:

> Hospitality is not to change people, but to offer them space where
> change can take place. It is not to bring men and women over to our
> side, but to offer freedom not disturbed by dividing lines.*
>
> NOUWEN, HENRI J. M.

Reaching people with the Good News of the Gospel is not just a ploy to grow the congregation. It is not just something we should do because people might finally be warming to the idea of church. Reaching people is the heart of the congregation because it is the heart

---

* Nouwen, Henri J. M. Reaching Out: The Three Movements of the Spiritual Life. Doubleday, 1975, p. 71.

of the Lord. Does anyone doubt that Jesus' mission was to "seek and save the lost," as he said?

Before we suggest new programs or ways to welcome and involve new people in our congregations, our churches need to see the people of our community as Jesus saw those in his. A congregation that wants to grow must first want to care about others as Jesus did.

We must have a heart like Jesus' heart.

ABOUT THE AUTHOR

 David Roseberry has been an ordained Anglican minister for over 40 years. He was the founding Rector of Christ Church in Plano, Texas for over 30 years. Currently, he is the Executive Director of the non-profit ministry of LeaderWorks which serves congregations and leaders in the Anglican Church in North America. He is a preacher, bible teacher, and speaker with a growing ministry through his numerous books. Check out his Amazon Author page.

He also leads life-changing pilgrimages to Israel and other historic places of the Christian faith. Join us! Information is available at the LeaderWorks website.

He and his wife Fran live in Plano, Texas. They have five children and five grandchildren.

Stay in touch with the ministry of LeaderWorks.

ALSO BY DAVID ROSEBERRY

DEEPEN YOUR SPIRITUAL LIFE

The Ordinary Ways of God: Inside the Book of Ruth.

The Last Will and Testament of the Apostle Paul, Faith, Hope and Love: Enduring Truths for Challenging Days

The Psalm on the Cross: A Journey to the Heart of Jesus through Psalm 22.

When the Lord is My Shepherd: Finding Hope in a Hard Time. (available in Spanish)

The Giving Life: Why it is More Blessed to Give than to Receive.

The First 24: One Man. One Mission. One Day — Jesus of Nazareth

BOOKS ABOUT LEADERSHIP

Giving Up: How Giving to God Renews Hearts, Changes Minds, and Empowers Ministry.

A Field Guide for Giving: Increasing Generosity in the Local Church

Inspiring Generosity: The 10-Step Program for Highly Successful Annual Stewardship Campaigns

The Rector, the Vestry, and the Bishop

Authors who publish books independently rely on readers to offer honest reviews on platforms like Amazon or Goodreads. Please take the time to tell others about this book or any others you have read. Your comments are deeply appreciated.

If you have questions or suggestions about this book or any others, please contact me at David@ LeaderWorks.org. All of these titles are available at bulk rate discounts. Contact me for more information.

Made in the USA
Columbia, SC
27 January 2025

52821194R00074